Praise for 1314

One of the coolest publishing imprints on t...

These are for the insane collectors out there who appreciate fantastic design, well-executed thinking, and things that make your house look cool. Each volume in this series takes a seminal album and breaks it down in startling minutiae. We love these. We are huge nerds—*Vice*

A brilliant series...each one a work of real love—*NME* (UK)

Passionate, obsessive, and smart—*Nylon*

Religious tracts for the rock 'n' roll faithful—*Boldtype*

Each volume has a distinct, almost militantly personal take on a beloved long-player...the books that have resulted are like the albums themselves—filled with moments of shimmering beauty, forgivable flaws, and stubborn eccentricity—*Tracks Magazine*

[A] consistently excellent series—*Uncut* (UK)

The nobility—and fun—of the project has never been questioned...a winning mix of tastes and writing styles—*Philadelphia Weekly*

Reading about rock isn't quite the same as listening to it, but this series comes pretty damn close—*Neon NYC*

The sort of great idea you can't believe hasn't been done before—*Boston Phoenix*

For reviews of individual titles in the series, please visit our website at www.continuumbooks.com and 33third.blogspot.com

Also available in this series:

Dusty in Memphis by Warren Zanes

Forever Changes by Andrew Hultkrans

Harvest by Sam Inglis

The Kinks Are The Village Green Preservation Society by Andy Miller

Meat Is Murder by Joe Pernice

The Piper at the Gates of Dawn by John Cavanagh

Abba Gold by Elisabeth Vincentelli

Electric Ladyland by John Perry

Unknown Pleasures by Chris Ott

Sign 'O' the Times by Michaelangelo Matos

The Velvet Underground and Nico by Joe Harvard

Let It Be by Steve Matteo

Live at the Apollo by Douglas Wolk

Aqualung by Allan Moore

OK Computer by Dai Griffiths

Let It Be by Colin Meloy

Led Zeppelin IV by Erik Davis

Armed Forces by Franklin Bruno

Exile on Main Street by Bill Janovitz

Grace by Daphne Brooks

Murmur by J. Niimi

Pet Sounds by Jim Fusilli

Ramones by Nicholas Rombes

Born in the U.S.A. by Geoffrey Himes

Endtroducing... by Eliot Wilder

Kick Out the Jams by Don McLeese

Low by Hugo Wilcken

In the Aeroplane Over the Sea by Kim Cooper

Forthcoming in this series:

London Calling by David L. Ulin

The Notorious Byrd Brothers by Ric Menck

Loveless by Mike McGonigal

Doolittle by Ben Sisario

Daydream Nation by Matthew Stearns

There's a Riot Goin' On by Miles Marshall Lewis

Stone Roses by Alex Green

Court and Spark by Sean Nelson

Music from Big Pink

A Novella

John Niven

2009

The Continuum International Publishing Group Inc
80 Maiden Lane, New York, NY 10038

The Continuum International Publishing Group Ltd
The Tower Building, 11 York Road, London SE1 7NX

www.continuumbooks.com

Music from Big Pink is a work of semi-fiction.
While real people and events are described, certain conversations
and scenarios have been imagined by the author.

Printed in the United States of America

Library of Congress Cataloging-in-Publication Data

Niven, John, guitarist.
Music from Big Pink / by John Niven.
p. cm. -- (33 1/3)
ISBN-13: 978-0-8264-1771-8 (13-digit pbk. : alk. paper)
ISBN-10: 0-8264-1771-X (pbk. : alk. paper)
1. Band (Musical group) 2. Rock music--United States--History and criticism. I. Title. II. Series.
ML421.B32N58 2005
782.42166'092'2--dc22
2005019642

One

"Don't you raise the sails anymore..."

Toronto, 1986

I don't know why I was crying like that. I hadn't seen the guy in years and he hadn't crossed my mind in months. But here I was, standing right in front of the Mini Mart, reading the newspaper and bawling my fuckin' eyes out. The stuff I'd just bought—canned soup, Wonder Bread, turkey roll, processed cheese slices—spilled from the dropped brown bag and rolled over the sidewalk.

Sitting down heavily on the curb (I'm in my forties and weigh nearly 300 pounds: I do everything heavily these days) I stared at the photo in the *Star* of a gaunt, bearded Richard. I looked at the headline again, hoping the words might have changed in the last few seconds. That "DEAD" would somehow have become "ALIVE." Or "PARTYING." But it hadn't. It still said:

"BAND" SINGER FOUND DEAD IN HOTEL ROOM.

Suicide, it said. He'd fuckin' killed himself. Richard had done that. He'd killed himself. I kept right on crying. I'd had a shitty week and hadn't seen this coming. I'd just had an argument in the grocery store—the guy who runs the place accused me of passing him a bum bill. (I hadn't, although I had twice before, getting away with it the first time and around it the second.) Anyway, we wound up getting into it. I was on an economy drive until the welfare check arrived at the end of the week and hadn't shot up since breakfast. It was now late afternoon and I was jerking, man: my sweat just froze in the early March breeze.

After a while an old girl stopped and—this being Canada—asked if I was OK. I looked up and caught my reflection in her Foster Grants: the rotted teeth, the starbursts of broken blood vessels across my yellowing cheeks. Neither of us needed to be seeing this. Bravely, like a child, I sucked the sobs down and nodded. She handed me a dollar and walked on. I wiped my face with a ragged shirtsleeve, gathered up the cheap food, and hurried home.

The place was a living shit-house. It had taken my parents thirty years to own it and me just three to run it into the ground. I would have drawn the shades but they were already drawn. I did the thing with the spoon and the lighter, the brown powder and cotton ball, the old hypodermic. (Glass and steel, pre-war, my father's.)

The heavily treated guitar came in like an ancient tramp wheezing his last, then the woody toms, deeper than a crack on the floor of the Atlantic. I took my shirt off, found a halfway decent vein, tied off, put the needle in, and pressed the plunger. I turned the old stereo (also my father's) way up, lay down on the rug, and let the intro go through me as I started to glow; the tempo of the song good and slow, slow as memory, the beat of my heart. Finally, here was Richard's voice, trembling in fuckin' agony; "*We carried you in our arms, on Independence Day.*" He sang the words the way he'd sung everything: as though the information contained in the lyrics would end him.

I stared into the black rippling pool of the speaker, feeling every tremor and pulse like breath on my face, wondering if over the years the fibers of the cone itself had somehow become stained, impregnated with the thousands of songs, the millions of notes, that had shivered as they passed through and out into the air: electrical impulses becoming sound that became meaning and heartbreak. I turned away and looked up. It took me about a minute. There was a crack in the ceiling above me and, like magic, a tiny fleck of plaster broke loose and came floating down, like a sorry kind of snowflake, or maybe a leaf.

Sixteen bars, a spoonful of Iranian heroin, and I was two decades back into myself, floating happily through another time, another place. A time when we were all making money, driving good cars through the mountains, getting high, getting laid. A time when we were all living, not just waiting. Life is all just waiting after a while.

Two

"It's for sure..."

New York City, 1967

It had been a long, long Friday and I hadn't left Fifth Floor Dave's place in Alphabet City until after seven o'clock. It had also been a real hot day and it seemed like tonight every joker in Manhattan with access to a fuckin' automobile was trying to get out of the city and up to the Catskills before the summer called it quits.

There'd been a smash up ahead and I spent a goddamn frustrating 45 minutes trying to get onto the New York State Thruway north of the island, all the while surrounded by the usual highway trash: unsmiling businessmen in Oldsmobiles and Caddies, hippies in Volkswagens, the necks of acoustic guitars juttin' out the windows, "Lucy in the Sky with Diamonds" blaring out their AM radios. Next came the station wagons jammed with bawling kids and their sweating folks, all trying not to kill one another. (Now that's a good one, ain't it?

"Hey, the five of us don't get along in a *house*. Why don't we all cram into a 110-degree, eight-foot space for a few hours?" Great idea, Pop.)

Above us all sat the truckers in their fuming eighteen-wheelers; grim-faced, identikit pedophiles in mirrored Aviators and coffee-stained vests, caged 20 feet up in their chrome porno-rooms, their jerkin' off boxes. I mean, these guys, pumped up on bennies, caffeine and Marlboros, these guys jerked off *while* they drove. They were the kind of people who laughed and yelled stuff about your hair when you walked into a diner. ("*Hey, are you a boy or a girl?*" Suck my dick and find out, you stupid fuck.)

As I was trying to change lanes some girl in a Camaro bawled me out for cutting her up, yeah cutting her up at three fuckin' miles an hour, and I nearly jumped out and got into it with her boyfriend. But then I remembered all the shit I had in the glove box and thought better of it.

Two hours later I took the Saugerties exit off the Thruway, pulled over to put the top down, and drove on, heading west on Route 212. I loved this part of the drive, when the smell of the Catskills hits you right in the face—clean, fresh air washed and scented by the maples and pines. It would be October next week. Fall sets in early in the mountains and its first murmurs were visible—splashes of rust and coppery fissures running here and there through the leaves. Overlook Mountain loomed in the distance and somewhere at the foot of it was Woodstock.

I had been living in the town since the previous summer, the summer of '66, the summer Dylan had his little spill over there on Striebel Road. I'd had some trouble down in the city and my friend Alex said I could come up and stay for a while.

I'd left Toronto to come and study law at NYU a few years earlier (about the same time The Hawks were playing behind Ronnie Hawkins and really packing them in down on Yonge Street; but our paths never crossed) but college and I didn't really get along. After a couple of years I was pretty much done with it and was running speed and grass around Manhattan for a guy called Manny.

Manny was into a few things. He used to sell drugs to a lot of the Factory people, ran some numbers. He had a few girls on his books. Not what you'd call a stable—just a few broads who worked Times Square, draining the balls of the convention-attending jerks who flew in from the Midwest, the kind of guys you saw wandering around Midtown at night frazzled on scotch and soda, guys whose wives back in Minnesota hadn't fucked them right since Truman was in the White House, and who didn't complain too much when the cowgirl-style riding they'd been promised on the street wound up being a 30 second handjob in the room. It was the same old story: these girls—the daughters and nieces of the scotch-and-soda-30-second-handjob Mr. Joneses—would get off the bus downtown thinking about Broadway and meeting Merv fuckin' Griffin, until the 200 bucks they'd saved up working at the Dairy Queen back in cow-town ran out. Then they'd meet guys like Manny. Within a few months they'd be shooting speed and smack, nodding out under those hot lights with the 16mm camera whirring away and six or seven cocks going off in their faces. I heard that later on a couple of Manny's girls actually got TV shows and stuff, but most of 'em would wind up just getting older and skinnier and junkier until they found themselves turning forty down in the meatpacking district, teeth gone, doling out head and hand to cabbies and dockworkers at five bucks a pop.

It was all cool for about six months. After a while, though, I'd made a few connections of my own and was sick of the twenty bucks here, ten bucks there, while Manny was making all the real dough. I mean, I was the one riding around town with ten years on Rikers Island rammed down the crack of my ass. So—classic cliché shit—I started doing some work on my own. Then one night Manny showed up at my apartment with a Mexican guy who could barely fit *in* the apartment. They slapped me around a little, then Manny said that if I sold my shit to his customers again his friend here would sodomize me then "nail my fucken balls to the table."

Well, fuck that. I bummed around on the money my folks were still sending for a few months—until they found out from a friend of a friend that I hadn't been near the NYU campus in almost a year. They cut me off. So here I was in this situation. I had no money. I had people I could get drugs from, but no one I could sell them to. And that's when Alex called from Woodstock.

He said rent was cheap, Tinker Street was crawling with folksy girls in summer clothes and there were enough people in town who wanted to buy.

Grass was easy to get and Alex had a pharmacy connection with a guy along the road in Kingston who could get us several varieties of fat chick pills. For the heavier stuff I made the run into the city once a month (although it was starting to get more like bimonthly) and saw Fifth Floor Dave or the black guys I knew over on 10th Avenue.

And you know what? Fuck it, I thought. Fuck Manny and his wetback rapist enforcer. Fuck my parents. Fuck New York City. My apartment—my twelve-foot-square oven—off

Canal Street was 300 dollars a month. Up here we were pay-ing 120 between the two of us for a three-bedroom house. The living room had 14-foot-high ceilings with cedarwood beams and a big fireplace built out of blue Catskills stone. There was an old knotted pine dresser in the kitchen. We even had a couple of acres out back with a porch and tacky-cool Adirondack furniture. Man, it was paradise, two hours north of the city.

I had put the car in the drive, tucked all the shit under my bed, and was popping the cap off a cold Heineken when the phone rang. The heel of my hand caught the bottle-top and tore a little flap of skin off. Tired and pissed, I snatched the receiver up. "Yeah?"

"Greggy?" No mistaking that croak.

"Hi Rick."

Rick was one of the few people who knew what I'd been doing down in Manhattan. He'd probably been calling for hours. "Hey man. You OK? I've been calling."

"Yeah, I just. I cut my fuckin' hand."

"Shit, be careful there. So, are we, um, happy?"

"Yeah, we're happy."

"Then come on over."

"Ahh, it's late. I just got in. Maybe we could..."

"Hey, fuck that. C'mon man. Bring your guitar too. It's just me and Richard and a few chicks."

I thought for a moment. I did have to drop something off at Bill Lubinsky's place. Old Bill was a good guy, a fixer, wheeler-dealer type; one of those guys who'd offer to get you anything from an M-16 to a T-Bird. He was also a little nuts—drove around with a loaded .45 under the seat. I think he'd been in the military and you heard talk around town about him being a mercenary, being at Bay of Pigs a few years back and stuff. But I don't know. Who knows? Bill lived up at the end of Pine Lane, not far from the band's place.

"You'll get your dick sucked," Rick said in a hoarse snigger. I could hear female laughter in the background, Richard shouting something.

* * *

"Greg! How you been?" Richard kicked the screen door open and we embraced as well as we could given that I was carrying a guitar case and a bottle of bourbon and he had a huge, badly made joint dangling from his lips, a glass of something in one hand and a can of Bud in the other. "Greg's here!" he shouted into the house and I followed him through.

The place was a mess. The ugly pink house had been gradually deteriorating since Richard, Rick and Garth moved in back in the spring. I'd stepped over a fresh dog link outside and Hamlet was stretched out on the rug having his belly stroked by a young, drunk blonde. The neon beer sign Richard had stolen from a bar downtown glowed on the mantelpiece above them and music—unusually it sounded like their music—played softly in the background.

"Greggy!" Rick bounded across the room. He too seemed more than happy to see me; then again drug takers (we weren't drug addicts, not yet) were usually happy to see you when you were bringing them stuff.

"How was the city?"

"Fucked. It took me an hour to get on the interstate."

"Shit. Well, you're here now. This is," he turned to the

two girls sprawled on the floor with the dog, "this is Shirley and...Marla?"

"Carla!" the blonde giggled.

"Carla, sorry baby."

They were both fuckin' cute. You hand it to these guys, they got girls, man.

"Hi," I said, setting down the fifth of Four.

"Hey, Greg," Richard smiled, raising one of those big, furry eyebrows. "Did you..."

"Yeah yeah." I pulled out two cellophane bags from my jacket pocket; the bigger one was full of grass (these guys got through a lot of grass) the smaller one was coke. Richard gleefully slapped them on the table.

"Oh, oh, and listen to this!" said Rick, jumping hyperactively across the room. "We just did this." He turned the volume up and the music cut through the blue dope smoke with unusual clarity. The songs they'd been recording down in the basement all summer didn't sound like this. I mean, they were starting to write some pretty good stuff, but the sound quality? Jeez. You hated to criticize people, but they were out of their minds recording down there. The whole room was concrete and metal; cinder block walls, a cement floor, a big iron furnace and these steel foundation poles. It was the worst possible environment to record in. I'd mentioned it to them once or twice, but they didn't seem to give a shit.

This was different. I listened—blown away but not showing it—as Richard sang a beautiful song about losing a girl called Katie. That voice. Man, he could break you up just singing the lottery numbers. I looked over to him and his eyes flickered up at me, bashfully. "You did this downstairs?" I asked.

"Nah. Down in New York a couple of weeks ago."

"Who's Katie?" asked Shirley. Or Carla.

"Robbie's mom," Richard replied deadpan, not looking up from the pile of powder he was smoothing across the back of a framed picture. Rick laughed—a short bark—and leaned in with a tightly rolled twenty.

Hours later Richard and I were sitting out back finishing up the liquor and watching the sky. We could hear Rick playing bad piano down in the basement, working the same chord progression over and over again. The talk all night had been about Levon, their old drummer. They hadn't seen him since he walked out on the Dylan tour nearly two years ago and they were thinking about getting him back up from down South to help with all the new songs. They'd heard he was working on oil rigs in the Gulf of Mexico or someplace.

"I don't get it," I said. "The guy just walks out on a fuckin' world tour to go be a deckhand or something?"

"Yeah, Lee's got balls!" Richard chuckled. "To tell you the truth, I don't think he really liked Bob's music too much." I couldn't understand this.

"As a matter of fact," he continued, "I don't think Levon liked Albert too much either." This I could understand. Grossman, Dylan's manager, was a scary, cold-hearted son of a bitch.

"So, you're gonna sign with Warner?"

Richard shook his head. "Capitol now, I think."

"How come?"

He shrugged. "Albert had some meetings. He called Robbie. Hell, I don't care. Long as we get the check!"

"How much do you think you'll get?"

"Fuck Greg. Like, a couple o' hundred thou?"

"Shit man."

We looked at each other and he burst out laughing. It was just too crazy. We laughed for a while then he looked out across the fields, pointed, and said, "Hey, look at that." I followed his trembling finger. In the distance the rising sun was hitting Overlook Mountain. "Man, that's fucking beautiful," Richard said.

He gazed out and put the bottle to his lips. I watched as he took a long pull; a pattern of early morning sunshine glittering off the emerald glass while the birds chattered in the pine trees around us.

"Shit," he said as he passed the whisky, "ain't life *good?*"

Three

"We spent our whole lives at sea..."

Dylan's arrival in town had made Woodstock about as cool as any place in the known universe. But in a low-key way—this was way before the festival and all the stupid shit that happened later when the hippies came.

I'd been up to his house once, toward the end of last fall, and it was because of that night that I eventually got to know the guys in The Hawks. Tommy, Alex and me had been drinking in Deanie's one Saturday night when this girl Chrissie, who we kinda knew but didn't like (she was beautiful—button nose, straw-blonde hair, Disney freckles, perky little titties—but a real star-fucker), came in and asked us if we could get any smack. I had a little in the house that I wasn't going to sell, but I asked her who it was for anyway.

"This film guy," she said, then added in a stupid, stagey whisper, "he's staying up at Byrdcliff. At Bob Dylan's place."

Twenty minutes later we peeled off Camelot Road and up Dylan's driveway. A sign on the gate said:

IF YOU HAVE NOT TELEPHONED, YOU ARE TRESPASSING.

"Shit, maybe we should have called."

"Oh, it's OK," she said casually. "Bob's not here. Didn't I say? He's down in the city with Sara for the weekend." I looked at her and thought, you fucking *cunt*. But I didn't say anything. Fuck it. Get to see the place anyhow.

We parked in front. Dylan's house was this huge chateau ("Turn of the century," said Chrissie, like a tour guide) built along the side of Mead's Mountain. A rambling, classy old place of cedarwood, stone and mahogany shingle. I followed her off toward a little outbuilding that looked kinda like a garage and I could hear music—Motown—coming from inside.

Chrissie pushed the door open. The garage had been turned into a poolroom where a huge, twitchy guy, maybe in his mid-thirties, and a younger couple were shooting some eight ball. The big guy shuffled over and held out a massive paw. "*Hi. I'm Howard,*" he shouted over the music. The couple—a stunning, exotic, dark haired chick and a tall, cool looking guy in shades and a sharp houndstooth check jacket, both about my age—nodded hellos but didn't really pay us much attention. "Come on," said Howard as he led me off, "let's go in the house."

You bond with people fast when you take dope. Fast and shallow. We'd snorted some of the smack—there wasn't much but it was really good; Chinese fuckin' crazy powder—and this Howard guy was talking and talking.

"What we're uh...excuse me, man...what we're trying to make here is something that'll really...really freak people out. It'll be like this trip that...where...where's ah, yeah...man, that is some nice junk you have there, some *nice* junk...where you from? Canada? The boys are all from Canada you know, I ...oh, here we are..."

He was messing about with reels of film that had been shot on Dylan's tour of Europe earlier that year; the one where people were losing their minds because he had a backing band with him. They had a machine (a Moviola it was called) set up in one of the bedrooms. It was like a big, metal reel-to-reel tape deck, but for film. It had a little TV screen on it and you could run the film back, forward or whatever.

In the car Chrissie had said Howard had been here a couple of months, working with Bob (again with the fuckin' "Bob") and trying to edit all this footage into an hour-long television special. The original guy who was doing it had quit over in England having been driven nuts by Dylan, and I think old Howard was starting to go a little crazy too, stuck up here on the mountain. What with the smack on top of whatever he'd been doing earlier, he was pretty wasted by this point. He ranted and raved as he rooted through those cans—boxes and boxes of them—until he eventually found what he wanted and started feeding the film into the machine. "Here. Look at this."

He pulled me toward the tiny screen. Footage of a steam train crossing the English countryside gave way to a bunch of fans shuffling into a Dylan show, then a brief shot of a wasted-looking Dylan in a dressing room somewhere, then back to another train shot, then some cops, then another show. It went on like this for a while, no one clip lasting for more than a few seconds. Man, you couldn't even hear the songs properly.

"You see what I'm saying? Each section, every sequence,

will fall together with a musical, an orchestral logic. In the same way individual notes form chords."

Shit, tell me these guys weren't doing drugs up here. The movie was a fuckin' mess.

"Err, yeah," I finally said. "It's pretty...radical."

"Hey, you're goddamn right it's radical. This is going to blow people's minds. Anyone can make a fucking documentary. That's why we had to sack Don. It's like I've been telling Bob, we have to..."

"I—sorry man—where's the john?"

"Oh, right across the hall there."

Lightheaded from the junk I waltzed off, grateful to be away from the yabbering and get a look around. The place was like a hotel in France or someplace. Antiques up the ass. A load of paintings—abstract, unfinished looking canvases—leaned here and there against the furniture, against the walls. To my left was this huge, dark living room. A little way inside an enormous book was opened up on a lectern. The kinda thing they'd have in a church. I tippy-toed over and stood there for a minute, wasted, just looking at it. A couple of pages were bookmarked and I turned to one: Revelations. As I was trying to figure out what this might mean for the next Dylan record a voice behind me said, "Can I help you?"

I turned. The guy from the poolroom—the guy in the houndstooth check jacket—was standing in the doorway watching me. The pointed, burning tip of a joint dangled from his lips and glowed in the shadows.

"Umm, no. I was just..." I gestured toward the lectern.

"Should you be in here?" he said evenly.

Fuck. "Sorry. I was only...I...like, who are you?"

He just smiled—an enigmatic, unfriendly smile—and

walked off. The fucking prick was real calm. From down the hall a girl was calling something to him in a French accent.

I went back into the Moviola room where my new buddy had some more footage up.

"Hey," he said as I walked in, "I got some foil here. It's a waste snorting that stuff."

On the screen Dylan was in a hotel room somewhere playing a song I didn't recognize on one of those new Fender acoustics. "We got hours of this shit to cut," said Howard. "Who needs to see another documentary about a bunch of guys playing the fucking guitar, right?"

The camera panned across to the other bed. Facing Dylan, looking sick as a dog, yellow as a Manhattan cab, and picking out an intricate lead part on an old Martin was the guy who'd just basically told me to fuck off. "Who's he?"

"Robbie? He's Bob's guitar player. You met him back there in the pool room."

"Riiiight," I said.

That was how I met Robbie Robertson.

The guy was cold.

* * *

I'm telling you, man, he was *cold*. None of the other guys were like that. Garth was a bit distant, but not in a mean way. He was just older and weirder than everyone else. Later on I figured out that Robertson's thing was something he'd gotten from Dylan, or Grossman, or both: that it's cool just to be, like, *silent* most of the time. You'd say something, something obvious or pleasant—like a couple of times I tried to give him some production tips, just a little advice—and he'd look at you from behind those pebble glasses like you'd fuckin' grown horns, man. Or just look right through you like you weren't there. Like Dylan did. But, the guy's guitar playing? Holy shit. I mean, forget about it. He was only the same age as me, maybe just a year older, but he could make that Fender fuckin' *talk* to you, man.

The first time I really heard him play, like up close and personal, was one night when a few of us were sitting around the living room at the pink house, everyone stoned and drunk and wasted and passing joints, bottles and guitars around. Robbie didn't hang around getting fucked up and playing tunes as much as Rick and Richard and—later—Levon would. He had his old lady at home and he hung with Dylan and Grossman more than the others did, but he was there that night.

Richard was singing something, some Ray Charles tune (we all loved Ray Charles, and Richard could sing the shit out of that stuff), and there were a few of us sitting on the floor listening. Robbie was perched on a chair, nodding along, just listening with an acoustic guitar cradled in his lap, when, from nowhere, he leaned forward and just...*drilled* this fucking solo out. Shit, it was like a bird flying—his left hand swirling up the neck in a beautiful flurry, finishing on this real high note way up on the b string, his thumb and guitar-pick popping off the string together, making this unbelievable ringing, crying harmonic and bending the string so far I thought it was gonna bust. His right hand was raised up above the neck, fluttering in the air like a shot bird, while the left hand wrung the last bits of feeling from the sustained note.

One of the girls sitting cross-legged on the floor went, "Whoa!" I looked over at Bill Avis—my expression saying *what the fuck?* He just smiled. He'd seen it all before. But me...I mean, I was stoned and all, but, shit, my jaw was on the fucking floor. So, although we didn't really get along, I had to admire the guy. As a musician.

* * *

It was late now, up here in Bob Dylan's big old wooden mansion in the mountains. Howard and I smoked up the last of the junk—chasing the brown-black gobs around the sizzling foil with a yellow straw—and he put an old blues record on, Elmore James or something, while he did whatever he had to do with those rolls of film. I lay back on the couch, nodding out and in; the heroin making the music drip like molasses from the speakers, great slabs of bottleneck clanging and swooping over my head and swimming through my vision.

After a while Chrissie came and got me and I gave Howard my number and we left. She drove my car—the radio off, the top down and the blue night air all around us as the big Lincoln whipped by the Ashokan Reservoir. I was so high I felt like I could hear the pumps and valves humming beneath the surface, the uncountable pebbles and rocks clacking together as they sifted and moved beneath millions of gallons of clear mountain water.

Also down there, flaking and eroding on the reservoir floor, were the remains of the town of West Hurley where old Walter Travers grew up. He said it was the city's fault. In 1898 its boundaries expanded; Manhattan joining with the other boroughs to form New York City. One of the things New York City needed was a billion gallons of fresh water every day. So the men came up here. They had maps, geological charts, strange tools, instruments and vision. They commandeered ten thousand acres of Ulster County. They dammed the Esopus River. They cleared the Travers family and two thousand other people from their homes. Then they brought the water down: levelling West Hurley and ten other villages, covering 13 square miles and creating the Ashokan.

The water flowed downhill, through the Catskills aqueduct, through broad pipes sunk 300 feet beneath the bed of the Hudson, through Silver Lake and Staten Island, and into Manhattan, nearly a hundred miles away. The water flowed downhill, seeking its lowest level, seeking the city, while the artists and musicians flowed uphill into the mountains, seeking...well, maybe just seeking. There had been a real nice bakery in West Hurley too, said Walter.

I was smiling, stretched out there in the passenger seat, feeling like I'd made an important connection and enjoying being driven down through the dark hills toward town by this beautiful girl who I didn't really know or like.

Four

"I'm pushing age 73..."

There were a lot of people like us in Woodstock: kids in their early twenties with no responsibilities, a little money from doing whatever, and a taste for what Johnny Becker used to call "high quality mood tailoring ingestibles." Most of us came from different parts of the country, drawn to the town (usually via New York) in the summers by the cheap rent/nice houses/Bob Dylan combo. Alex and Tommy were from Ohio, Chrissie and her friends were Californians, Johnny B came from Detroit, The Hawks—except Levon— were Canadians, Warren and Jeannie were New Englanders. It was a real mix. You know how they say that Manhattan is this island off the coast of America? We all felt that we were like this island off the shore of Manhattan.

Johnny B was a real junkie, the first guy I ever saw popping a needle between his toes. But he was cool and fucking funny, super-smart and real sarcastic. He'd been busted on a dope possession charge in San Francisco in '66 and had jumped bail to run east. He was renting this little place off the Glasco Turnpike that had no heating, so he became a regular fixture at our place during the winter. Man, seeing Johnny B go at it with little Tommy—that was some funny shit.

We were all sitting around getting stoned one night and Johnny convinced Tommy that the commies were putting bromide in the American water supply. Just tiny amounts, nothing you could really detect, just enough, over time, to make you impotent.

"I'm telling you T, by the year 1980 this generation of American males will have dicks like acorns. We'll be ejacualtin' nothing stronger than fresh air."

"What's ejaculatin'?"

"He means coming, Tommy," said Alex.

Tommy looked at Johnny. Then at us.

"Naw, man. The guvver...the guvvermint would tell us if that shit was going down."

"Are you crazy bro?" said Johnny. "They'd start the biggest panic in history. There's nothing they can do about it now anyways. It's a done deal. The commies are gonna come marchin' in here in about twenty years and they're gonna start fucking your sister, boy."

"Goddamn it Johnny, I told you before, don't be talking about ma sister like that!"

Me and Alex were crying, man.

"Yeah, there's gonna be this big Red commie sonofabitch with a schlong like a nuclear fucking missile schtupping your sister, Tommy."

"Fuck you, man!"

We had to pull Tommy back. Johnny B didn't know where to stop.

Now and again my mom would call. I don't know how she got the number. She called one night when Alex and me were stretched out wasted in front of the TV watching *The Smothers Brothers*. She started with the stuff about what everyone had been up to—Uncle Whatever had fallen down the stairs, Auntie Who Cares had to have her fuckin' womb removed (like you ever needed to hear about that kind of shit, man)— before asking about when was I going back to finish school.

I told her I wasn't sure the law was for me. That I still needed a little time out to clear my head. That I was thinking about—maybe—re-enrolling for another course next year, in the fall '68 semester.

"Maybe pre-med," I said.

Alex hooted—not at the *Smothers* show—and I threw a softball at him. "Y'know; like Dad," I said, not making it sound one way or another, but really knowing this would terminate the conversation pretty fuckin' quickly.

"Yes, well that would be wonderful Greg. But it's a lot of work you know, medicine."

"How is Dad?"

"He's fine." Yeah, right. "He sends his love."

"Listen, I gotta go, mom."

"OK. Take care of yourself."

"You too."

Alex tossed the softball back to me with the words "You, my friend, are a nasty son of a bitch" and started rolling another number.

Was I going back to school? Like fun I was.

Some weeks in the summer I was clearing four, five hundred bucks straight profit a fuckin' week. I was on first-name terms with people like Paul Butterfield and The Hawks. Even

Dylan had nodded at me a couple of times. I had three or four different kinds of weed under the bed, a shoebox full of amphetamines and barbiturates in the closet. I had a little ceramic honeypot with a fat, happy bee on it on the top shelf of the dresser in the kitchen. I kept the junk there. "Time for a little honey," we'd say.

The news was on now, the same stuff you were seeing every fuckin' night: those big Huey's coming down in dusty clearings, body bags, maps, and troop statistics and stuff. My dad had been through this stuff. An army doctor, bouncing around islands in the Pacific in '44 and '45, coming in behind the Marines as they cleared out the Japs. His main job was popping enough morphine syrettes into kids to stop them screaming for their mothers while they bled out. One for pain, two for eternity, they used to say. Guys could still scream for a long while with four or five shells the size of a shot glass studded across their chests.

We weren't worried. I was Canadian—this shit with the slopes had nothing to do with me, man—and Alex was medical exempt on account of only having one kidney (or so he claimed). But Alex was worried for Tommy, probably because Tommy didn't have the good sense to be worried for himself. His number was getting low. He didn't even have college to fall back on. "What are you gonna do if they call you up, man?" I asked him one night. Tommy thought for a second.

"Man, old Tommy will be smokin' in Alaska so fucking fast you won't believe it."

"Uh, Tommy, Alaska is still, like, in the US," said Alex.

"Ain't it Canadia?"

"No, man."

"Ain't part of it in Canadia?"

"Shit, no Tommy."

"Damn. Where *is* in Canadia?"

"Vancouver? Quebec?"

"Yeah, that's what I meant. Vancoooover," he strung the word out, enjoying the sound of it. "You watch. I'll haul ass up there, man. Sit tight in Vancoooover. Don't you boys go worrying about old Tommy."

We were laughing our asses off, man.

According to Alex, Tommy's high-school SAT score was something like 211. Just 211. Shit, is that even possible?

* * *

I loved those goofy weekends up in the Catskills. On a Saturday afternoon Alex and me would sit out on the porch, grilling hamburgers, drinking beers, rolling joints: we were a regular counterculture Ozzie and Harriet out there with the barbeque, the Adirondack chairs, the smell of charcoal and pine.

Our place was just a few minutes from Tinker Street, so people would drop by, some of them picking up pills and powders and feel-good shit for the weekend, some just to say hi and hang out. Sometimes friends would come up from the city, although I didn't really encourage the likes of Fifth Floor Dave too much; I had a good thing going up here and I didn't need those guys moving in. (But they wound up coming anyway, by end of the decade there were probably more dealers than guitar players in Woodstock.) We'd all hang out in the yard getting stoned and throwing the football around until it got dark, then we'd stumble along the road to Deanie's and get ripped.

It was right after Halloween and we were out back having

one of those Saturday afternoons—taking turns shooting up our jack-o'-lantern with Alex's .22 Woodsman—when a VW Beetle came clunking up the drive and Warren, this friend of Alex's from the city, got out with these two girls.

Two girls? Man, these two exotic looking creatures. The first one was a screech of red hair, a slash of orange lipstick. The second one was dressed head to foot in white Biba: billowing white shirt, thin, white cotton pants, head-scarf, white mules. She had coal-black bobbed hair, a bottle of Rolling Rock in one hand and a cigarette—in a thin black and gold holder—in the other. She looked about eighteen years old, looked like she'd stepped out of *Vogue*, or a Truman Capote book, or a fuckin' Dylan song. I thought, *You gotta be kidding me, Warren.*

She was skipping toward us, laughing at something the other girl was saying, when she tripped up and went fuckin' *flying* into the muddy lawn, the beer bottle catching on the cement path and exploding like a glass hand grenade. We ran to help her but she was flat out on her belly, howling with laughter. It took her a couple of minutes to get up. When she did, she was just destroyed. I mean, this chick had totally fuckin' obliterated herself in the space of two seconds—she'd cut her hand open and she was covered in blood, mud and beer. "Fuck, are you OK?" I said.

She wiped her palm on the seat of her pants, raking a huge bloodstain across them, before daintily offering her hand to me, "Hi, I'm Skye," she said. "Could I trouble you for a beer? A Rolling Rock if you have it?" Her accent was beautiful; pure Vermont, New England old money. I looked down at my hand, her blood all over my fingers. I was *gone*, man. Just real cornball love-at-first-sight gone.

Later, after we got her cleaned up, bandaged, and changed into one of my old T-shirts and Levi's, we all went out to Deanie's. It was rammed, bluegrass playing and waitresses going back and forth with steaks and chili. We were slamming tequilas and chasing them down with cold beers, all talking at once, the way you do when you're full of new people and speed and infatuation. Skye was nineteen, a sophomore at Columbia. We talked about Paul Butterfield's band and about the downers she'd gotten from her mom's bathroom cabinet. She knew her music and her drugs. She had a little beauty spot high up on her right cheek.

On the way to the john I ran into Rick at the bar. "Greggy! What's going on, man?"

"Ah, just pounding a few."

"Hey, come by our table. You gotta meet Levon."

I squinted across the room, through the smoke and music. A bunch of the guys were all around a big table in the corner: there was Avis, Richard, Howard, and a couple of guys I didn't know. One of them—lean, bearded—was telling a story, cracking the others up.

"Yeah, man, I'll come over."

"Who you with?"

"Uh, Alex and Warren and..." I gestured vaguely toward our table.

"Shit, man, who's the fox?"

Fuck. "Uh, Skye? I think she's...like she's Warren's girl-friend or something."

"Fuck. Bring her by."

"Yeah, sure."

Man, I didn't need cooze-hounds like Danko and Manuel

fucking this up for me. But what can you do? They all wanted to meet the guys who played with Dylan so we went over
and joined them. Levon, the drummer, the new guy, was a few
years older than the rest, in his late twenties, and he was a real
life, no-shit, Southerner. I'd never met one before. He started
sentences with "Well, son," and finished them with "Yessir."
You could have listened to him all night.

"Greg gets the best pot around here," said Richard, intro-
ducing me.

"Is that a fact?" said Levon. "Tell me son, have you ever
come acrawss some weed called Chicago Green?"

I said I'd heard of it.

"Shit Greg, that there is some serious mary-jew-anna."

"Yeah?" I was a bit distracted. Over the other side of the
table Rick was listening to Skye. Her face was animated, lit up,
as she explained something to him.

"Hell yeah," said Levon. "Trust me on this one. I've
smoked weed from New Orleans to Anchorage and that
Chicago Green is the finest pot in the Yew Ess. If yew can
ever lay your hands on some I'd sure appreciate it."

"Yeah, I'll call a guy I know."

"What you drinking there son?"

By midnight everyone was pretty totalled. The place had
emptied out some and a few people, regulars, were ragging on
the guys to sing something. A guitar and a mandolin appeared.
While they tuned up I went and sat down next to Skye.
"Having fun?"

"You bet. I didn't know you were so connected," she said,
patting my leg kinda playfully.

"Oh, I'm full of surprises."

Levon said, "Well folks, this here is a song ma daddy

showed me," and they went into it.

"Ain't no more cane, on the Brazos."

It was a song I'd heard before, an old chain-gang number recorded by Leadbelly, but it sounded like nothing I'd heard in my life. Levon was playing mandolin, Rick guitar, all three of them singing harmony on the opening chorus. It was the first time any of us had heard the three of them sing together, and their voices just fit perfectly. It was just the rawest sounding thing I'd ever heard from white men. There were people like Paul Butterfield doing this kind of stuff but, these guys, I guess with Levon being from the South and Richard having that Ray Charles thing, it was black-blues-white-country-soul all at once, man. Levon took the first verse, his eyes shut and his head down as he flailed at the little mandolin, the veins in his neck standing out as he growled out this song written decades before by some black guy who couldn't read or write.

"You should have been on the river in nineteen and ten.
They were driving the women, just like they drove the men."

He sang in the most perfect extension of his speaking voice. I thought this guy was the drummer, but here he was —playing mandolin, singing great. These guys, man, it made you wanna do something to yourself.

Richard took the next verse, his voice catching, quavering with hurt in his throat.

"Oh mister don't ya do me, like you done poor old Shine.
You drove that poor boy till he went stone blind."

I glanced to my left. It was like she was watching the second coming or something.

Rick took the last verse, singing it shamelessly right at Skye, and then they all brought it home together, letting the last almost-in-tune chord ring out true. As the applause started—instant and sincere—Richard scooped up his glass and drained off about a half pint of dark liquor, crunching the ice cubes, hanging his head in shyness. I sometimes wondered what it cost him singing those songs the way he did. Like, just singing for some friends and a few strangers in a bar he'd wring everything out of that lyric, chasing the melody through that high ghostly register he had.

They started closing up the place. No one was gonna follow that. Richard invited us back up to the pink house and suddenly we were out on the street in the rain and there was the usual hubbub of who was going with who and people were pulling on coats, climbing into cars. I looked around just in time to see Skye getting into Rick's Continental (The Confidential, he called it). The car was already full. Shit. Richard was getting in his car alone, but I wasn't getting in there. No way. No one was gonna ride with Richard, the way he drove.

Levon came out behind me with this girl Bonnie. He looked at the rain coming down. "Hell," he said. "Rainin' like a cow pissin' on a flat rock. You need a ride, son?"

I watched as Danko's car peeled off—Skye and Warren waving to me from the backseat—and nodded. Levon followed my gaze. "Shit, I guess we'd better get you back there quick. I wouldn't be leevin' young Rick alone with that one for too long!" I climbed into the passenger seat, Bonnie got in the back, and we took off behind Richard, his red taillights already disappearing into the distance. Somewhere ahead of him was Rick. "Don't worry; we'll catch 'em," said Levon, flooring it. We went hurtling out of town toward Saugerties, barrelling at seventy along those Ulster County backroads.

Levon was telling us about a motorcycle crash he'd had down in Arkansas recently (which wasn't exactly filling me with confidence) when we came to that sharp corner before Zena Road. It was a hard, downhill, left-hander. It dawned on me that Levon had only been in town a little while. "Hey," I said, "you might wanna..."

"Ah know, son," he flashed the lights to see if anything was coming round the corner headed in the other direction. When he got no answer he just floored it and we came screeching around the bend about as fast as you could without going off the road. Bonnie screamed.

I saw it all very fast: the cop car parked in the middle of the road, red and blue lights strobing in the night, Richard and the two cops right beside it, Richard's car nose-down in the ditch behind them. They turned, wide-eyed in our headlights, Richard shouting something and them leaping out of the way. Levon started to brake, but he realized he couldn't stop in time. So he just slalomed through everything: the cops and Richard and the cars. He almost made it too but then our front just caught the back of the cop car at about fifty miles an hour. I balled up and shouted "*Fuck!*," then there was breaking glass, crumpling metal, and Bonnie screaming as the car spun across the road.

We came to a stop ass-way round; facing back along to where the cops and Richard were scrambling out of the ditch they'd jumped into. Man, we'd nearly killed all of them.

There was broken glass all over the car. Levon got out shaky and headed over to Richard.

"Are you cut?" I asked Bonnie. She shook her head numbly.

"I don't think so."

I could see from here that Levon had demolished the police car, just smashed it to fuckin' pieces.

Bonnie was picking shards of glass from out of her hair and I was just getting around to thinking about how bad it would be if these cops searched me when Levon came back and perched down on the driver's seat. I could hear one of the cops shouting something to him.

"Are you guys all right?" he asked me.

"Yeah, are they OK?"

"They got a damn good scare. I..."

The cop grabbed hold of Levon's jacket and just tore him out of the fuckin' car, man. I had only known the guy a few hours but I'd already sensed that he wasn't the kind of guy you'd put your hands on.

Sure enough, Levon grabbed ahold of the deputy and ran him backwards, the two of them swinging and flailing at each other, pumped from the accident. Richard and the other cop ran over and the next thing you know the four of them are going at it like one of those crazy cartoon fights—fists and legs and heads and all of 'em rolling around in the wet gravel. "What the fuck, Greg?" said Bonnie.

I crammed the big bag of grass and the speed into the glove-box and got out, running across the road just in time to see one of the cops pull a mean looking blackjack out. As I shouted "Hey!" he brought it down hard on the back of Levon's head. He went straight down. This was fucking over, man. Richard put his hands up, saying, "OK, OK."

They cuffed them and took them off to the station and Bonnie and I finally got up to the pink house at about four a.m. Everyone had left or gone to bed. There was a T-shirt on the floor. My T-shirt. A little further along were my old Levi's. Further still, at the foot of the stairs, was a pair of white cotton panties. There was a tiny bloodstain on them. I stood at the foot of the stairs and listened. Sure enough—it wasn't a huge house—I could hear it all going on in a bedroom upstairs, Rick and Skye.

Five

"There's only one place was meant for me..."

Winter bit down hard and early, like it did up there.

You saw cars skidding across Tinker Street, people getting stuck in their driveways and the Ashokan freezing up around the edges. A guy Bill Lubinsky knew got me some chains for my tires; Cream released *Disraeli Gears* and Woody Guthrie died.

I was kicking around at home one night when Michelle, this girl who worked for Grossman, called and said that Albert was having a little get together and that they were a bit low on certain "party elements" (man the shit people talk when they're being coy about drugs on the fuckin' phone) and could I swing by? Grossman got through dope like he got through all that gourmet fuckin' food he liked so much and I heard talk he sometimes hit the harder stuff too. He'd come out of that whole Chicago, Second City scene: people like Howard, Del Close. Lenny Bruce too. A real heavy junk scene. Grossman scared the shit out of me. He was fuckin' huge (they called him The Bear), clever, rich, intimidating. I mean, Dylan could be sarcastic, withering, aloof—all that stuff—but, I'm telling you, from what I saw he was Charlie fuckin' Brown next to Albert Grossman.

But, to tell you the truth, I wouldn't have minded getting closer to the guy. He was big league—as well as Dylan and The Hawks he managed Janis Joplin, Peter, Paul and Mary, Paul Butterfield—and there were rumors he was gonna start his own record label soon. Maybe I could get one of the guys to give him a tape of some of the tunes I'd been recording at home. Also, it was business and I needed the money, so I got in the car and drove over to Bearsville, where Grossman had a big estate. Yeah, we all thought it was pretty fuckin' funny that The Bear actually lived in Bearsville.

There were about twenty people there: Richard, Rick, and Levon, this guy John Simon who was a friend of Howard's, Paul Butterfield and a couple of the guys from his band, Chrissie and a couple of girls I didn't know, and a few people who worked for Grossman. The room was grand and softly lit, lots of rich wood, heavy drapes, and logs crackling and spitting in the fireplace. Like Dylan, Grossman had antiques coming outta his fuckin' ass: rugs, vases, lamps, paintings; all kind of tasteful, expensive-looking shit.

Over in what was obviously the power corner was Grossman, Robbie and his wife Dominique, and a couple of guys I didn't know. I did the thing with Michelle and was standing having a drink with Butterfield and Richard. Butterfield was asking Richard about the Guthrie tribute thing that was coming up at Carnegie Hall.

"What songs you gonna do?"

"Shit, Woody Guthrie songs I guess. I don't know if we're

all gonna do it even. Maybe just Rick, Robbie, and Lee."

"You should do 'Grand Coulee Dam,'" I said.

"Yeah, well, it's Bob's call," said Richard, picking up a frosted bottle of fancy vodka from a side table and hefting it in his hand, as though gauging the quality of the contents from the weight. He poured a long shot into his glass.

"What's happening with your deal, man?" Butterfield asked.

"It's happening," said Richard, looking across the room to the power corner where, wreathed in smoke and strangely colored by the greenish pool of light spreading out from an ornate lamp, Grossman was gesticulating with a cigarette and shaking his head, his heavy Benjamin Franklin jowls lolling, as he explained something to a nodding Robbie. Robbie had his hands clasped in front of him, like he was in church or something.

The night went on, everybody smoking a lot of weed, drinking up a storm. Butterfield and Levon were singing a number and I was sitting in a corner talking to Richard when I looked up and saw Howard Alk and that fucker Bobby Neuwirth walking into the room.

They were trailers, man. The main feature came through the door a beat behind them.

People redistributed their weight when Dylan came into a room. You saw them shift their footing, cross their legs, press back in their chairs. Or slip a hand into their back pockets, nod harder at something that was being said, suck more air than they needed into their lungs and laugh harder than the jokes deserved. A lot of people suddenly found real interesting marks on the carpet, fascinating spots on the walls, and cool reflections in their drinks but, if you'd looked, you'd have seen he had on a blue cotton shirt, cream pants, and brown moccasins. His hair was short and neatly backcombed and he was squinting behind wire-rimmed glasses. From where I was sitting, cutting your hair, having kids, and going to bed at night looked like a good thing, man. I mean, Dylan looked healthy and fresh, nothing like the wired wreck from a year or so ago, the guy in Howard's documentary.

There had been this scene in the documentary: Dylan in a cab with John Lennon, driving through a gray English dawn. They'd obviously been up all night and Dylan looked like he was gonna throw up; tight-jawed, his hair greasy, his skin the color of cordite. His fingernails had been black, like they get when you've been fucked up and haven't slept in days and you've been running your hands through your hair and sticking 'em in your pockets and stuff. But the fingernails were clean now; they stood out trim and white, like little shells, against the ruby wine in his glass. If you didn't know who he was you'd have figured him for a lecturer at a rural college, or maybe a painter from Maine. Neuwirth sat down next to Robbie and Dylan sat next to Neuwirth—keeping a few people between him and Grossman, not even saying hello—and, after a moment, the party regained its regular heartbeat.

Richard was totalled now, drinking straight from the bottle. There was a coffee table in front of us—ashtrays spilling over, glasses with bursts of lipstick, a capo, a lacquered walnut box, joints in different stages of construction. Richard fumbled amongst all this stuff and found a pack of Marlboros. He lit one up and went on talking, talking about his family back in Stratford, Ontario. Richard had three brothers. His dad worked at an auto plant, his mom was a school teacher, and here he was—stretched out on a thick rug slugging on a twenty-dollar bottle of red in this mansion in the hills. Playing piano behind the biggest rock star in America.

Out of the corner of my eye, I saw Grossman beckoning to Michelle. She crossed the room and leaned down to talk to him, pulling her long blonde hair behind her ear to listen better to whatever he was saying. She glanced my way and then back to him. What the fuck? I kept my head turned toward Richard, but I was really watching them with my peripheral vision. You could never be too paranoid in this kind of company. Grossman was getting up now. It was taking a while—he was a big fuckin' guy and he was stoned and sunk deep down into that soft couch. With his frizzy gray hair, gray sweater, gray face, he looked like a cloud of smoke coming up. But Michelle put her hand on his shoulder and said something to him. He sat back down and she turned and walked across the room toward us.

"Greg, can I talk to you for a minute?"

"What's up?"

She looked around, kneeled down and whispered in my ear, "Look, I'm sorry, but Albert says you have to leave."

I looked at her.

"I'm sorry. It's just, it's a private party. You weren't really meant to stay."

Richard leaned in. "What's wrong, man?"

"Your manager says I have to leave."

He turned to Michelle and spoke gruffly. "Tell Albert he's with me."

"C'mon Richard, I'm sorry." She brushed her hair back nervously. "But you know what he's like about people around Bob."

"Greg's a friend. He ain't just fucking 'people.' And Bob don't give a fuck."

"It's OK, man," I said getting up. "I was gonna go into town anyway." I was glad of the lighting; my face was reddening.

"Thanks Greg. I'm...y'know," Michelle stammered. "I hate doing this."

Richard drained the bottle, set it down, and looked up at me. "You going over to Deanie's?"

"Yeah."

He got up unsteadily.

As we left, Dylan was laughing at something Neuwirth was saying, his head down and a cigarette smoldering between his fingers, like a fuse.

* * *

A few weeks after the car-smash, just before New Year's Eve, I was standing in line at the Colonial Pharmacy on a freezing cold Tuesday afternoon when somebody tapped me on the shoulder; I turned around and there she was—black hair tumbling out from under a furry logger's cap and wearing an oversize fleece-lined buckskin jacket and mittens. "Hi Greg!"

"Uh, hi. I thought you'd gone back home?"

"Yeah, I did. How have you been?"

"Good...yeah, good. What you up to?"

"I've just got to cash a check. Jenny and I decided to come down for a few days—we're staying up at Warren's folks' place. We tried calling you a couple of times."

"Yeah? What, did you want something?"

I didn't mean it to sound like it did. Or maybe I did.

Skye looked at me. "It was just to see if you wanted to, y'know, hang out."

"How's Rick?"

"I think they're down in the city," she said, looking around. "Recording or something."

I nodded and looked at the rows of mouthwash, saying nothing. I noticed how small she looked in this place, in those winter workclothes that were way too big for her. (And whose clothes were they?) I also thought how clever she looked, something about the way it seemed like she was fighting a smile the whole time, as if she had already thought this scene through from a couple of different angles and was two moves ahead while I was still trying to figure out the rules.

"So, what are you doing tonight?" she asked.

"Oh, me and Alex are..." Are what? What the fuck were me and Alex doing? "...We're going over to Kingston. To see this thing, uh, *The Graduate*?"

"Rilly?"

"Yeah." Yeah rilly, you fuckin' bitch.

"Can I come too?"

Un-be-fuckin'-lievable.

"Sure," I said.

The movie was about this uptight rich kid who winds up fucking this older woman, this WASP friend of his parents, and we loved it from the start: the kid, Benjamin Braddock, sitting on the airplane and then moving along that walkway with the song "The Sound of Silence" playing.

I mean I wasn't a Simon and Garfunkel fan or anything, but that song just sounded fuckin' *great*: a clear, ringing guitar arpeggio and vocal and then these amazing harmonies and a whole band kicking in. It rocked harder than any of their other stuff I'd heard.

I topped off our paper cups of Coke with a slug from a pint of bourbon I'd smuggled in and we toasted each other there in the dark. It felt great to be there—hunkered down in those plum velvet seats in that big warm, old theater while this movie you just knew was gonna be cool got started.

She hadn't seemed surprised when I drove over to pick her up without Alex and the ride over to Kingston had been a riot. Having Skye in the car was like having this psychotic nine-year-old on a fuckin' sugar rush or something. About halfway along Highway 28 she started in with "I wanna snow cone. I wanna snow cone."

"C'mon, you gotta be kidding me."

"...snow cone...snow cone..."

"Shit, Skye. It's, like, four degrees outside. What the fuck do you want with a snow cone? Let's get a cup of coffee."

She looked at me real serious and said, "Snow cone."

"Fuck, OK. Snow cone. *Jesus!*" But I was laughing.

"Yayyy!"

I pulled into the drugstore off Washington Avenue and Skye went in while I smeared this thick, syrupy hash oil I'd just gotten in over a couple of papers and made us a beautiful, moist, sweet-smelling joint.

I torched that mother up and sat gazing through the icy drizzle, through the window of the place, at this beautiful little chick running around inside, piling up stuff on the counter.

She took a while and when she finally came running back across the parking lot toward me I was smiling so much—lost in the fantasy she was my girlfriend—that I had to shake my head to get rid of it as she opened the car door.

"Grape," she said, handing me a frosty paper cup.

"Grape?"

"Grape. The only snow cone flavour that should be legal."

She found an oldies R&B station on the radio and we sat there listening to the Staples singing "Why Am I Treated So Bad?" drinking those stupid kiddie drinks and passing the jay back and forth—her face in profile all pink and green from the drugstore neon and Mavis and Pops' voices coming out tinny on the AM. We just talked about stupid, funny shit and neither of us mentioned Rick or The Hawks or Dylan or any of that stuff so everything was fine.

Man, the older people in the movie were all like my parents' friends—well, like the friends they used to have. There was this scene where Ben's parents are throwing him a graduation party and this sleazeball guy is advising Ben about his future, and he throws an arm around the kid and says, "Plastics, Ben. Plastics." I was laughing so hard, just tears running down my face. Skye was looking at me and laughing at me laughing.

The colors of the fish in Ben's aquarium—orange and yellow, pink and green—were so fuckin' vivid. "*Oooh, they're beautiful little fish,*" Skye said. Then, when Mrs. Robinson's husband comes in and he's a little tight and giving Ben a drink and clamping his arm around him and getting in his face and all that? I felt like he was breathing scotch all over *me*.

I don't know. Either the sound in the movie or the sound system in the theater was incredible. Mrs. Robinson took her earring off to take a phone call. She slapped it down on a glass-topped table and there was this rattle of metal against glass; like it was happening right next to your ear. I whispered to Skye, "*Doesn't this movie sound incredible?*" She giggled, nodding, and took my hand.

Ben was smoking a cigarette and suddenly I wanted one

too. I lit a Camel and watched the silver-gray plume of smoke go drifting away—up into the darkness above us, heading deliberately for this one point of light I could see in the ceiling, like the last star in a black sky.

Then, about halfway through, there was this montage scene where "The Sound of Silence" comes back in. Well, shit. If I thought it sounded good about a half hour ago now I was thinking—"*Fuck, man! This is just the greatest song ever written. This is the coolest fucking movie ever made.*"

It cut from one image to the next, the song building and building ("*And in the naked light I saw…*") and then it finished and Ben was alone, just drifting there in the pool under the California sun. I could feel the sunshine on my face and smell the orange groves. The water in the pool glittered like liquid jewels, just the bluest water you'd ever seen. It looked to me like it was about to start pouring out of the screen and flowing down the aisles. I felt like I could fuckin' taste the chlorine. And now the red velvet drapes at either side of the screen were starting to, like, billow and furl, swirling like columns of fire up the walls.

A man sneezed a few rows away from us and I saw the sneeze blast out of him, ricochet off the screen, and go zinging around the theatre like a vapor bullet.

Fuck, man. No hash oil was *this* good.

I turned to Skye. Her eyes were bottomless black wells, her lips, purple-blue from the grape drink, were luminous.

She looked at me, at my open mouthed, bewildered expression, and then leaned in close, smiling, and whispered in my ear, "*I put a splash of liquid acid in the snow cones.*"

Ah fuck.

It was like her just telling me about it gave the drug the all-clear to go open-season on my ass: the acid started wheeling properly through my veins—fired up by all the sugar in the Cokes, the candy, and the snow cone; by the bourbon, and the hash oil—and the movie became as real to me as if I were sitting in those folks' houses. Ben goes round to the Robin-son place and finds out that Mrs. Robinson has told Elaine she's been fucking Ben, to stop her from seeing him.

I stood up in my chair and screamed "You fuckin' *CUNT!*" at the screen. As angry as I've ever been, man. A couple of people behind us yelled stuff and the guy came running around with the torch.

Skye was *howling*—having herself the best time ever.

By the time Ben was banging on that glass wall at the church I was fucking *feral.* The wedding guests were all shouting up at him. They all looked like these fuckin' Nazis: a sea of blonde-haired, blue-eyed Aryan supermen with sharp, ultra-white teeth, teeth like sandsharks, all spitting and gnashing at this poor little Jewish guy. The eyes and the teeth all flashing blue and chrome.

I was twisting in my seat, whimpering, "*Get out Ben, get out, man. They're gonna kill you!*" The camera swung onto Mrs. Robinson's face, her fangs bared like an angry rat.

She was the devil—evil personified. I cried out—"*RUN, BEN! GO!*"—and tried to throw the bottle of bourbon at the screen but Skye, her face soaked with tears of laughter, grabbed my arm and clamped her hand over my mouth. Someone a few rows back threw a candy box at me.

Then they were out and they were on the bus and it was over and the camera lingered on Ben's face, on that expression. It was...what? Relief? Fear?

I didn't know. I just didn't know.

Skye took my hand and lead me gently out through the lobby. Christ knows what we must have looked like, this laughing girl helping this stumbling, crying, bawling wreck. I turned to her and spluttered through the tears and stuff.

"Will, will they be happy?"

"Who?"

"Ben and Elaine. Will they make it?"

We stepped out into the street, into the snow, and she reached up to me and started drying my eyes with her sleeve. "Yeah, sure they'll make it. They're in love. Now, stop worrying, relax, take a big breath, and we'll go have some fun."

I exhaled deeply, feeling the tug of all the uncried tears still caught in my chest and throat.

"Aren't you out your fuckin' mind, Skye?"

"Fuck yeah!"

She took my face in her hands and looked right into my eyes. "Greg, the reason you're upset is because you think you're like Ben—a young man who doesn't know what he's going to do with his life. That it's all going to fall apart any minute. It's all going to be OK, y'know. Just run with it baby. Don't fight it."

I looked right back into her eyes and saw for the first time that they were green. I couldn't have told you what color they were before. She smiled and kissed me on the cheek.

It took us about an hour to drive the fifteen minutes back to Woodstock—the road, night, and cars like a movie being shown on the windshield—and by the time we got to her place I was just beaming, totally content. Skye poured brandies and laid me down on the couch.

Warren's folks had an incredible hi-fi, real top-of-the-line shit, and I watched as she threaded a reel through the tape machine. "You've got to hear this," she said.

She laid down on the floor, there was silence, then tape hiss, then all at once there was piano, organ, drums, guitar, bass; then Rick's voice, gentle, restrained.

> *"Bessie was more than just a friend of mine.*
> *We shared the good times and the bad..."*

A stately, graceful rhythm uncoiled, with Garth's organ rippling through, bursting out to fill spaces and then falling away into the shadows of the track when the vocals came in. The chorus welled up and I realized the song was about the old blues singer Bessie Smith. It sounded to me like nothing on earth and, at the same time, like it'd been recorded a hundred years ago and dug up out of the ground. The mix was kind of muddy and rough and the vocals a little swamped, but you could catch the odd chunk of lyric and when I heard Rick sing *"The best thing I ever had,"* I shut my eyes and felt my skin scrunching and puckering up in all the places it did when music was this good.

There was this perfect chord rundown and it was finished, the last notes on the woody piano and organ hanging in the air, fading like glory. We both laid there breathing. After a moment I said, "How could I not have heard that song before?"

"They only just did it."

"No, I mean the original version."

"What original version?"

"I mean, who wrote it?"

"Rick and Robbie," she laughed.

It took about thirty seconds for this to sink in.

"You are fuckin' kidding me," I whispered, not knowing whether to laugh or cry. But she didn't hear me. She was already rewinding the tape, getting ready to play it again.

It blew my mind apart that these guys we knew—guys who lived down the road from us, who were much the same age as us, who were really a bunch of backing musicians—were capable of writing songs like that. I mean Dylan, you figure that's just a different order of human, someone who falls from the fuckin' stars once every thirty years. But the guys in The Hawks...eighteen months before they moved to Woodstock they'd been playing the same kind of shit-holes around Toronto that me and my friends had played in, cranking out "High Heel Sneakers" and "Walkin' the Dog" for drunken assholes on a Saturday night.

I'd heard bits and pieces of the music they'd been making with Dylan down in their basement all that summer. Up by the Revox next to Garth's organ there were stacks of tapes—mostly cover versions, or twelve-bar jams with Dylan rambling over them, takes on songs by people like Johnny Cash, Hank Williams, Elmore James, all of them really badly recorded with a couple of shitty mikes. A lot of what I'd heard sounded like real stoner stuff. Like comedy music. The kind of shit guys with guitars do when they're getting wrecked and giggly. So, that winter, when we finally started to hear some of their own songs, it was kind of a shock. It was as if you had this friend who said they were writing a book and you go, "Yeah, sure you are buddy," and then they turn up with the great American fuckin' novel under their arm. It was like that.

I got home around dawn, still pretty mangled from the acid, to find Alex sitting on the sofa drinking neat whiskey and smoking a big jay.

"Hey, man," I slurred, struggling out of my big winter coat.

"Uh, your dad called."

Huh? "My fuckin' *dad* called? Are you drunk, man?"

"It's not cool, Greg."

I saw now he was looking right at me.

That's how you get dramatic news. That's how you hear the big stuff. Not in some emergency room, or sitting down face-to-face with someone all serious. It's when you're pulling off a shoe, changing channels and lighting a cigarette, or reaching for a can of spaghetti in the kitchen cupboard. The phone rings, or someone comes through the door looking at you funny, and that's when you get told. So I'll always remember pulling my coat off that night, the night Skye spiked me, the night I really heard The Band—as opposed to The Hawks—for the first time. It was a real cold, blue December night, with the new snow all pearly outside and the stars way up in the sky and now my mother was dead.

Six

"Oh to be home again..."

The guy, the pilot, said we were headed north-northwest, so I guessed the brown and green squares down below us were maybe Pennsylvania. Flying was nice. It had cost me a bunch, sure, but I was good for money and I figured that, if I was going to go through with this, I might as well do it right.

I feasted on my vodka-rocks and looked around at all the other guys who were doing it right: crew cuts, suits, and polished shoes. Argyle socks, gold tie pins, and the smell of shaving lotion. They called the stewardess things like "sugar" and "sweetheart." She was a porno-looking blonde in her late twenties, could probably have been a model if she hadn't been a little bit cross-eyed. I was decent enough to her—I called her "Miss" and stuff—but I was the one she looked at like a hunk of dog shit. I guess she couldn't get her head around the fact that someone younger than her, someone who looked like a deadbeat, was on her turf. When I came on the plane—panting and sweating from running—she'd read my ticket slowly, like it was in fuckin' Japanese, and looked me up and down three or four times. I'd run like a madman all the way to the gate. I swear, sometimes it felt like you were taking your fuckin' life in your hands whenever you stepped outside Woodstock and into the world.

I'd gotten to LaGuardia early—Alex driving me down, he was borrowing my car and taking care of business while I was gone—so I'd jumped into a bar to pound a couple. It was one of those thrown-together corners of fake wood panelling and caramel Naugahyde; packed, smoky, and noisy. I took a stool at the bar. The barman was an old black guy with a big, fat face, a face you'd normally imagine being cheerful. But today he looked like he was under pressure, sweating through his white polyester shirt. A waitress came up to him, Chinese, in her late thirties maybe. Probably pretty once, but it looked like it had been a long, hard day on top of a long, hard life; her hair was plastered to her forehead, she held a tattered pad in her left hand and a wet tray dangled from her right. "They want four more pitchers and another round of tequilas," she said, sounding tense, like you would, getting minimum wage, getting stiffed on tips, getting hit on by drunken assholes all day.

"They had enough," the barman said, not looking up from pouring a beer.

"Well why don't you go and tell 'em that, Bernie?"

Bernie sighed and looked across the room. I followed his sad stare. In the corner, underneath the football game purring from the big TV, was a group of maybe a dozen Marines in full dress uniform. Their luggage, their green canvas knapsacks, was stacked up around their table like sandbags. They were dug in, man: talking and laughing loud, their tanned, shaved heads clustered in tight together, like the ball players in a huddle on the screen above them. Only these guys were bigger. One of them, a huge mean looking son of a bitch with a vicious fresh scar crawling up the back of his head like a pink worm, stood up excitedly in the middle of the story he was telling and made like he was holding a machine gun, miming firing it, yelling *"Motherfuckers!"* The others were all laughing their asses off.

I mean, fuck. Over here, these were guys who wouldn't get a job at the fuckin' 7-Eleven, the kind of guys who sat out on their back porches shooting up bottles and cans. Over there, they were God Almighty. One of them, just a kid, maybe twenty, looked me up and down, taking in my scuffed cowboy boots, raggedy jeans, untucked check work-shirt, and my hair. Shit, my hair wasn't even that long—I'd had a few inches cut off it right after I saw Dylan up at Grossman's place—but this kid was looking at me like I'd turned up to take his sister to the prom with a bottle of Ripple wine in one hand and a pack of ribbed Trojans in the other.

Old Bernie didn't take too long weighing it all up. "Ah, fuck it," he said, reaching for the Jose and putting a fresh, frosted pitcher under the tap. "What'll it be pal?" he asked, flattening a cocktail napkin on the bar in front of me and wiping his forearm across his brow.

"Can I get a beer and..." I looked at the wall of hard liquor behind him; green glass, clear glass, brown glass. They still had their Christmas decorations up; little green paper trees, red baubles, and silver tinsel hanging around and through the bottles. A sparkly gold and red sign above the register said "HAPPY NEW YEAR 1968." They looked sad, those decorations, like nobody noticed them except when they were squinting around trying to find their brand of whisky. "Uh, a double vodka?"

"Ice?" I nodded. "Those fellas hitting it pretty hard?" I asked him, nodding over to the gang of Captain fuckin' Americas.

"They been drinking all morning." He shook his head sadly. "Lotta flights delayed on account of the snow. Every day now, these guys, they get into Kennedy then some of 'em come here to get back to Iowa or wherever. They been in-country, Christ knows what kinda shit they've seen. They don't give a shit. Last night? I had one of 'em take a piss right on the goddamn bar. What am I gonna do? Take on a platoon of GI's? No Sir. Not for a dollar five an hour plus tips I ain't."

He put my drinks in front of me and went back to pouring the tequilas. I knocked the vodka back quickly—tasting just cold and burn—and lit a cigarette, the half 'lude I'd taken in the car earlier mixing quickly with the booze, making me happy and woolly: I was already pretty loaded and planning to go all the way, man. No way was I getting through this trip straight.

I hadn't been planning on going, no fucking way. I'd even told my dad I wasn't coming. "Well Greg," he began. "It's...if that's..." a pause of about five seconds, "...your, ah, *choice?*" He sounded like he didn't know what the words meant, like he hadn't spoken in a couple of years. I finally hung up when his silences started stretching to more than fifteen seconds. ("Hello?" he'd suddenly asked at one point, as if he was answering a call, as though he'd just realized he had the receiver in his hand.)

But people had talked me out of it. Richard said, "You gotta go home and bury your mom, man. It doesn't matter what shit you got going on with your Pop." Levon was more direct: "Don't be stupid, son." The guys in The Hawks were all real fond of their families. I thought it was kinda strange, most people around our age did nothing but bitch and moan about how their folks didn't understand them, didn't support them, but I guess because they'd all been so young when they left home to go on the road—Levon had been sixteen, Robbie only fifteen when they started traveling with big Ronnie Hawkins—they felt maybe they'd missed out on a part of growing up.

I was signalling Bernie for another round when there was a crash and a roar from across the bar. The Marines were all standing up shouting at the TV, there was some news report on: anti-war protestors in DC, shots of hippies chanting stuff in front of the White House.

"*LOVE IT OR LEAVE IT YOU FUCKING ASS-HOLES!*" One of the soldiers shouted. Another threw a shot glass at the screen, but missed. It smashed on the wall behind.

"Hey! Come on guys!" Bernie pleaded.

Yeah, time to go. I jumped outside and had a look at the board. It was only a half hour till my plane and I thought about what I was going to do when I got to Toronto. Go round and see Ritchie? Get a hotel? Go see my dad? A sick lurch of depression went through me with the last thought.

I jumped back into the bar to grab my bag. One of the Marines, the big, crazy motherfucker with the scar, was straddling my seat, leaning across the bar and arguing with Bernie.

"Here's the fucking money, just gimme the fucking bottle!" He threw a bunch of bills over the yard of wet mahogany and gestured for the tequila.

"I'm sorry Sir, I'm not allow—"

"Listen you sorry fat nigger..." he started ranting. The guy was mangled, man. Probably airlifted outta some jungle hell-hole less than 24 hours ago, been living on bark and bugs and axle-grease for months, and now here he was—back in the world and not getting what he wanted. From across the room he'd been scary-looking: up close he was fuckin' terrifying: six-two/six-three, easily 250 pounds. The stitching on the seams of his jacket was stretching, almost splitting open trying to keep him inside.

"Call the cops, Bernie!" said the waitress.

"Shut the fuck up, you gook bitch," said another one of the Marines.

I reached around the scar guy to try and pull my bag off the seat but he turned round, stumbled round, and our eyes met. I saw now that the scar came all the way around his skull and a couple of inches down his forehead, like someone had tried take his brains out with a fuckin' can opener. He had a big, flat Midwesterner's face and there was nothing in his eyes but hate. Search. And. Destroy.

"What's your fucking problem, hippie?"

"Ah, nothing, man. I'm just trying to—"

"What? *What the fuck did you call me?*"

"I didn't—"

"You see *these,* motherfucker?" He pointed to a shitload of ribbons on the breast of his uniform. His name—"Bannerman"—was stitched there too. I pictured his folks back home waiting for him: Mom and Pop Bannerman, sitting on the crumbly porch of some dustbowl farm drinking lemonade and watching for the bus to come blowing along. Then I felt the hatred of his stare again and it was harder to picture them. Who could have spawned this guy? Some murderess who'd been gang-banged by a couple o' dozen rapists? Anger getting pumped into hatred, gelling together to produce this hulking motherfucker. I nodded, my peripheral vision shimmering and narrowing, like it does before a fight, but, within it, I could see old Bernie, all urgent on the phone. "I got these defending your fucking ass," his trembling finger hovered over the ribbons, "so don't be calling me 'man,' boy."

"Sorry, my mistake."

"You're goddamn right it is," he pointed to the TV screen. "You one of these fucking peaceniks we been seeing on the tee vee?" He pushed me. "You one of these faggot sons of bitches been calling us baby killers?" I didn't say anything, just reached over again to try and pick up my bag. Bannerman put his hand—a side of beef—on my arm and leaned down close, his breath like meat and diesel.

"You wanna know something?" he asked, lowering his voice, his face inches away now, staring me right down. "I did kill babies. I killed me a bunch of them little yellow bastards. I shot 'em, I threw 'em in rivers, I burned the motherfuckers up. What you think about that, boy?"

"Hell," I said, looking in the mirror above the bar and seeing the four rent-a-cops piling into the place behind me, feeling Quaalude, vodka, and beer rippling through me, feeling like I didn't give a fuck anymore, "I'm just surprised you didn't screw 'em too, you fuckin' faggot."

His face worked fast, crunching through its gear-changes—scowl to puzzlement, to fury—in the two seconds it took him to believe I'd said it. In those two seconds I hopped back a couple of feet and the cops moved forward as he leapt for me. Three of them held him—just—as I ran for my gate, my boots slapping on the clean marble floors of the new LaGuardia terminal as I disappeared among all the Mr. Joneses with their briefcases and newspapers.

Now the Mr. Jones across from me was getting another scotch and soda—"*whythanchewlitteldarlin*"—while I got ignored. I'd pressed the button, even though she was only, like, ten feet away from me. Eventually she came over and turned off the little light above me like I'd been wrong to turn it on in the first place.

"Uh, can I get another vodka please?"

She smiled a tight smile, a game show-host smile, took my empty plastic glass, and disappeared. Finally, when there was no one else's paper to fetch, coffee to top off, or pillow to plump, she brought me the drink.

"Thanks."

"No problem," she said, managing somehow to make it sound like "I hope you get fucking cancer."

I drank half in one go and pressed my forehead against the window. It was real cold and my temples went numb as I watched while down below the brown of Pennsylvania turned into white, then, up ahead, the freezing black enormity of Lake Ontario. I had Richard's voice in my head, singing "Georgia On My Mind," a song about yearning and home-coming—"*In peaceful dreams I see…*"—and, what with the booze and stuff, I started feeling syrupy and sentimental. For just a second or two I lost myself up there in the sky over the border and started to feel like I wanted to go home, that I wanted to see the folks and walk the streets. Then the pilot's voice came on, telling us to buckle up, that we'd be landing soon, and I snapped right out of it, thinking about what a cheap, powerful shot music was and how stupid it was that one guy singing about wanting to go home to a place he didn't come from could trick another into thinking he wanted to go back to a place he couldn't wait to get away from. Outside the little scratched Perspex window the air rushed past; American sky, silently becoming Canadian.

Seven

"With my very best friend..."

"But some of them, man, you just wanna break their necks. I'm telling you Greg, kids now? They're way crazier than we were back then. Way crazier." Ritchie worked open two fresh Black Labels. It was the kind of domestic beer with no tab, the kind where you had use an opener to bust a little triangle on either side of the can. It reminded me of sneaking beer when we were kids. Mr. Dunlop bought it in bulk. "Shit, it is so good to see you again," Ritchie said again as we clunked cans, "five fucking years, man!"

Sometimes, like when he swore, you heard the Scottish growl come into Ritchie's voice. His dad moved the whole family here back in '49, right after he got out of the air force. Ritchie was only five, he doesn't remember much about Greenock, the place back in Scotland he grew up in, but Mr. Dunlop would sometimes call it "that shite-hole." He loves it here, man. Mr. Dunlop thinks Canada is fuckin' paradise. "You boys," he used to say, "you don't know you're bloody born." It used to crack me up, watching Mr. Dunlop walking proudly around his house, surveying his domain. Man, houses in Scotland must be pretty small for him to think his little place in Scarborough was paradise. He'd answered the door to me like it had been five days, not five years. Mr. Dunlop was a cool old bastard: he liked jazz and soccer and was about the only one of our parents who had not only let us practice in their house, but who actually seemed to enjoy it. (I remember one time he'd popped his head around the door after we'd finished shakily grinding through some Chuck Berry song—we were about fifteen—and said "Magic boys! Really great!" I'd tried to picture my dad doing the same, but it was like trying to imagine Ed Sullivan fucking.) Mrs. Dunlop and Ritchie's kid brother Steven had come through too and said how sorry they were about my mom, Mrs. Dunlop hugging me and saying over and over that it was "trah-jik, jist trah-jik son."

Ritchie was all grown up now, a high school teacher. We were in the den in the basement, drinking, catching up, and listening to the new Dylan LP, *John Wesley Harding*, which had come out a couple of weeks before. He'd only just got it. The new Dylan record felt just right to me: it was as bare and stripped and bleak as the January trees in the Catskills, just acoustic guitars, brushed drums, and his voice, soft, peaceful, and maybe a little tired, as he sang his simple truths and twisted aphorisms. Sure enough, some of the words could have come right out of the Bible I'd seen in his house that night. Rick had said that Bob wanted the guys to put some overdubs on the record when he came back with the masters from Nashville, but Robbie had listened to the tracks and talked him into leaving it like it was. I wondered about telling Ritchie this, but I didn't want to sound like an asshole.

I looked around the room, at the old battered couch with a tartan throw over it (a "shawl," the Dunlops called it), the lime green carpeting, still with a black stain, faded to ash now, where Ritchie had dropped a can of model paint fifteen years ago, the stupid, goofy Niagara Falls coasters on the little coffee table. I liked it down here. "I didn't even know if you were still living here, man."

"It's just for another year. Clare and I are saving up to put down a deposit on a place."

"How's she doing?" Ritchie and Clare had been together since, like, the eleventh grade.

"She's good. She's working at her dad's office now."

Ritchie's bass—a real nice '58 Precision, sunburst, rosewood neck—leaned in the corner, a thin coat of dust on the scratch plate. I remembered the day he bought it, back in the summer of '60; a year's pocket money, birthday and Christmas in one go. We sat on the bus back home with the heavy Fender across both our knees, then came down here and looked at it for hours, the sunlight flashing on the chromed pickup cover (before we knew you should take it off to play rock and roll) and the smell of wood polish. "Hey," I said, pointing to it, "still playing much?"

"Naw. Oh, except a few of us played at Pete Duggan's wedding last year."

"Shit, Pete got married?"

"Yeah, I know! Well, he kinda *had* to get married..."

We laughed. Pete "the meatman" Duggan had been one of the wildest of our buddies. One time, in junior high, he'd shit his pants on purpose, to win a quarter off each of us.

"Hey," Ritchie said, "do you remember that time he shit his pants for a dollar?"

"Man, it wasn't even a dollar. There were only four us there *including* Pete. It was, like, 75 cents."

We laughed for a while. Then we stopped and just sipped our beer, each of us trying to think where to go next, whether it was better to dust off another anecdote, to scratch around among the roots of our friendship, or to move on and ask a question about our lives now. I pointed to the cover of *John Wesley Harding*, the picture of Dylan with a couple of the Baul's, these crazy, funny Bengali musicians that Grossman had brought over to Woodstock. "Hey, you know that photo was taken along the road from our house?"

"Really?" said Ritchie. "Wow. Have you ever seen Dylan, like up close?"

"Yeah. Matter of fact, I was at a party with him a few weeks ago."

"Fuck off!" I just sipped my beer. He saw I wasn't joking. "Shit. What's he like?"

"Bob? He's...cool. Quiet, y'know? Takes his kids to school in the morning. He's into, uh, painting and stuff now."

"Shit, Greg. You and Bob Dylan. Fuck, man!"

"Ah, it's no big thing. Everyone's real friendly down there."

"Wow. Does he get fucked up?"

"Nah, not so much. He's more like a family guy now. He smokes weed."

"You've smoked weed with Bob Dylan?"

"Sure. A few times. Speaking of which..." I patted my pocket.

"Ah, I'd love to Greg, but I gotta work in the morning, man."

"Man, you got responsibilities now, huh?"

"Yeah, well, you know..." he laughed.

We fell into another silence and into the silence Dylan sang:

"Oh help me in my weakness,
I heard the drifter say.
As they carried him from the courtroom,
and were taking him away."

We both listened till the song ended and the needle bumped and clacked in the run-out groove, like it had thousands of times when we were kids. As Ritchie got up to turn the record over he asked me, "So, when you gonna go see your dad?"

"In a while I guess."

"It's kinda hard to believe, isn't it?" he said sadly. "Your mom going before your pop. What with everything..."

My mom's heart had given out on her. It was something in her family. Her heart was no good to begin with. Or maybe it had just had too much to do over the years. "Yeah," I said, working the opener into another can, "it sure is."

"You know, I saw your dad a few months back. Over in the park."

"Yeah? How was the good Doctor?"

"Shit. I don't think he recognized me, Greg."

I set my beer down on the table and gestured toward the dusty Precision, "Here, gimme that fuckin' thing over. You still got a guitar somewhere? C'mon, let's play a couple of numbers for the folks back home."

* * *

The snow was thick and still falling gently; all along the street I could see blips and dots of it passing through the soft white balls of light that fuzzed out from the streetlights.

I was a little drunk, weaving slowly through the suburban streets I grew up on, my ears numb and throbbing. It was nearly midnight now and the houses were mostly dark, the odd bright window casting yellow-orange light out over white lawns. Almost no two houses in Scarborough were the same. There were big mock-Tudor mansions, narrow three-story places, some wood frame houses, some red-brick. There were little bungalows, built right after the war, for veterans. The stretch of land I was passing had been an adventure-land building site when I was a kid. Now there was a row of neat little starter homes filled with families starting out, people like Ritchie and Clare. It made me kinda sad that Ritchie was going to wind up spending his whole life within a few hundred yards of where he grew up. Not me, man. At least I was out there in the fuckin' world.

It took me nearly half an hour to walk the quarter-mile from the Dunlop house just off Kingston Road to my folks' place down near the lake. My folks' place? My dad's place now.

I stood under one of the bare maple trees across the street and looked up at the big old house I hadn't seen in years. The green paintwork was chipping and peeling. A stretch of guttering hung loose above the living room window. Garbage bags were piled up along the side. You could already see the place beginning to shift, moving reluctantly from my mom's time to my dad's time. The wind chimes she had hung out on the front porch hung silent and motionless in the still, freezing air.

I looked up at my old bedroom window on the right-hand upstairs corner of the house. It was in there, nearly ten years ago, under the covers with my little plastic transistor radio, that I found out that by some freak of atmosphere, some miracle of wavelength and wattage, you could pick up WLAC out of Nashville. They had DJs like Hoss Allen and John R, guys who didn't play top forty, who played these strange, crazy swampy records you couldn't hear any place else—stuff like Jimmy Reed and Dale Hawkins and Bo Diddley. This dirty, filthy music. "Nigger music," my mom said. Records that crystallized out of the twists and coils of static; pulsing and crawling from the little two-inch speaker next to your head, reeking of sex and menace and the South. It got you to thinking about what went on down there, what life was like on the other side of Lake Ontario. By the time I was seventeen it was a done deal—one way or another I was headed to America. Going to college was just a way to get the plane ticket. It wasn't just me—thousands of Canadian kids had the same thing going on in their bedrooms; Robbie Robertson over in Cabbagetown, Richard up in Stratford, Rick in the Simcoe tobacco belt. They were all listening to that crackling AM signal and thinking about getting out, getting away.

I stood there for a long time, sucking freezing air into my lungs, my exhaled breath misting up into the dead elm branches above me, cold flakes falling into my hair and onto my face, stinging and icy at first, then warmer, melting, dripping down my neck, running inside the collar of my sweater. Remembering the nights when the yelling and screaming would reach a pitch of such intensity that my mother would run out the front door and I'd hear him crying and screaming up in his room. She'd come back—an hour, half an hour later—and run upstairs and it would all be quiet again.

A light went on upstairs, in their—in his—bedroom and a shadow fell across the yellow wallpaper and, before I knew what I was doing, I was running back up the street, back toward Kingston, slipping and stumbling in the slush and snow. Then I was in a bar. Then I was in a taxi heading west, heading back downtown.

* * *

Less than an hour after I'd stood outside my father's house I was laying on a big bed ("Queen" size) with a joint in my mouth. I watched the smoke curl up to the ceiling for a while, the only light in the room coming from the mint-green Holiday Inn sign glowing just outside my window, and then I got up and dialled his number. I told him my plane had been delayed: on account of all the snow. I said I'd get an early flight in the morning and see him there. He told me the address of the place and I wrote it down on a sheet of hotel stationary.

I hung up and looked at the piece of paper. The Holiday Inn was "*proud*" to serve you." Shit, man. They weren't just "happy" to do it, or "pleased" to do it. They were fuckin' "*proud*" to serve me. So I got on the phone and had them do just that. The kid who brought the cocktails up was about the same age as me, so it was a kick to stuff a twenty into his breast pocket and watch his face light up.

"Thank you sir."

"No, thank you my friend." He left and I lit into the first of the three Long Island iced teas I'd ordered. Out of nowhere, right outta left field, I was *happy* all of a sudden. I felt like I'd gotten away with something. It felt like Saturday morning. Like the last day of school. I flipped on the radio and got Dino singing "Little Old Wine Drinker Me," drawling it out like a dirty joke. I turned it up and danced over to the window singing along.

I looked out over the Toronto skyline. The snow had stopped and it was a clear night, big moon low in the sky. Lots of new buildings were going up. Man, it was like they were trying to turn the place into New York City—there were the beginnings of a couple of skyscrapers over toward where Yonge Street was, bleak metal fingers clawing up into the moonlight. I remembered something from when I was little, someone telling me how long Yonge Street was—"*the longest street in the whole wide world.*"

I changed stations, looking for some rock and roll, and heard a DJ saying, "And now—Canada's NUMBER ONE RECORD!" and then the Stones doing "She's a Rainbow" filled the chintzy little suite. I did a stupid Jagger jig across the floor as I knocked back the last of the cocktail and grabbed the next one off the cart, spilling some.

She was holding my hand and telling me that I had be very careful and stay really near her, because it was so big and I might get lost.

The Stones finished and the DJ was talking shit, so I flipped again, looking for something loud and fast. I relit the joint and got some static, then Jim Morrison bawling "Love Me Two Times," but it was just finishing so I churned on around the dial, getting static, talk shows, advertising...

Then she was picking me up and carrying me along because it was so busy and I was only five or six and she was scared I'd get trampled.

The Stone Poneys cut through the fizz singing "Different Drum"—"*You and I marched to the beat of a different drum*"—the girl's voice so clear and direct and now I wasn't dancing anymore. I was standing looking out the window, remembering.

Remembering the smell of her hair and the feel of the fur collar of her winter coat against my cheek as she carried me along and I could see

right over all the people, all the way down Yonge Street. I said it was a
big street and my mother told me—"that's right sweetheart, it's the longest
street in the whole wide world," and kissed the tip of my nose.

I didn't want to remember but I couldn't help it. So I
stood there for a while up at the window, thinking about my
mom and not drinking my stupid cocktail with the Stone
Poneys playing in the background.

* * *

I got there early and had the cab driver park across the street
so I could watch the people gathering outside the funeral
parlor. There weren't many: over the years my dad had managed to whittle their circle of friends down to less than a
handful. There was Mrs. Durning, and a couple of other old
broads who'd been colleagues of my mom's way back when.
There was my Aunt Jacqueline and Uncle Mort (my mom's
sister and her husband) and a bunch of my cousins. I didn't
recognize a few of them because they were just kids the last
time I saw them and now they'd swelled up into pudgy, sour-
looking teenagers. But I recognized Jackie's son Frank—that
dickhead—and his sister Trudy. Shit, little Trudy. She'd been
about thirteen when I left Toronto. She was eighteen now
and a fuckin' fox. When had I last laid eyes on all these people? I remembered: Thanksgiving dinner '63 at Jackie and
Mort's. A few days after Kennedy got shot.

"You on a stakeout or something?" said the cabbie.

In terms of my dad's friends I could only see old Dr.
Callaghan, who looked like he should be the one getting
buried. I couldn't see my dad. Finally they all filed in. I paid
the guy and hurried across the street.

I went through a little vestibule that smelled of dead flowers, dry Bibles, perfume, and polished wood. Looking through the clear section of a stained glass window set in the main door I could see my father sitting alone on the front right hand side pew. My mom's family were all behind him, ignoring him, and my mom's friends were all on the other side, ignoring him. Dr. Callaghan sat right at the back, kind of apart from it all. I pushed the door open.

Callaghan, the man who'd delivered me, turned and gave me a warm smile, reached out and patted my arm as I passed him. My Aunt Jackie looked me up and down, fuckin' horrified at my jeans, boots, and whatever. Ah, fuck you, you old cunt. My dad turned as I sat down beside him. Man, he looked like shit—real yellow skin, his eyes rheumy, the whites all bloodshot to hell. His hair, once a distinguished sweep of silver, was all brittle and frazzled and there was a film of dandruff sparkling around the collar of his black suit. He'd shrunk in the years since I'd last seen him, it was like someone had scooped out some of his insides and he'd just folded in on himself. Scrawny chicken skin hung around his neck in folds, like his flesh was a suit that was too big for him now. He looked like an old, melted candle and I wondered what it was taking out of him to be here. What was it costing him to be among all these people?

"Hello Greg," my dad said, then the minister came out and started talking and I drifted off into myself, feeling my breakfast—Valium and Smirnoff—kicking in. I looked up at the stained glass window in the back wall of the little chapel. Jesus, dressed in pale violet robes, a halo of peach glass behind his head, had his hand on the head of some guy—a disciple I guess, some Mark, or Luke, or John—who was looking up at him reverentially. Jesus was smiling back. Winter sun was coming strong through the glass, through the little squares and circles of ruby, gold, and blue. My parents had both been doctors, they weren't big churchgoers. Maybe they'd both seen enough people's final moments—pain, bargaining, fear, mess—to have their doubts about the soul. When I was a little kid and we had to go to church with school—at Easter and Christmas and stuff—I never felt anything other than bored shitless. Then, when I got older, I just stopped going, like everybody else. I thought that maybe today, with my mom in a box over there, and the crying all around me, and the booze and the tranquilizers in my blood, I'd feel something like you were meant to feel in church. But I didn't.

I came back into myself in time to see that we had to stand up. I helped my dad up and together we watched the coffin trundle back on some rollers, the clanking, metallic sound of the machinery audible, strange and alien over the music and the crying. The coffin went through the thick purple drapes toward what I imagined were the flames, but Garth Hudson, who had started out in music playing the organ in his uncle's funeral parlor, told me much later that it really went to a kind of storage area and that they burned the body later, I guess so folks wouldn't be walking outside and seeing flakes and crumbs of their loved ones blowing across the street.

* * *

The phone finally stopped ringing. I wandered back into the kitchen and looked in the fridge: there was a goddamn science fair going on down in the vegetable crisper. A block of

American cheese, its side studded with mould the color of rusted copper pipes, lay in the door shelf. One egg sat desolate and lonely in the door tray built for twelve. A half-full quart of milk, curdled thicker and more viscous than slush, was next to the big orange cast-iron pot, the same pot Clarissa, our maid, used to bring hot and smoking to the kitchen table in my childhood, saying *"Here we are!"* as she put down some gurgling, bubbling swamp of brown meat and vegetables. I lifted the cold lid on a sticky puddle of black gravy and bones. Something my mom had cooked weeks ago. I wondered if he was bothering to eat at all, then I saw the menu for Hong Wa's was taped to the kitchen wall by the phone.

The one thing he did have was ice, so I opened the cupboard above the fridge, clanked and rooted through the bottles, and found an unopened fifth of Ballantines. From far away in the house I could just hear the TV, crumpled applause and bursts of music, coming from his bedroom, where he'd gone for "a nap" when we got back. The ice creaked, splintering under the amber wash of the scotch, and the phone started ringing again.

After the funeral we were all meant to go back to Jackie's for coffee and sandwiches and shit, but I'd looked at my dad—crumpled, wasted looking, and exposed out on the street—and thought "no" while I said "yes" and pretended to listen to her directions. I hailed a cab and neither of us seemed surprised when I gave the driver our address. Now Jackie was ringing and ringing, probably more furious at the slight than worried about what had happened to us. I shut my eyes and held the glass over my mouth and nose—letting the fumes tear up my eyes and numb my nose, my throat—and, after a minute or so, the phone stopped.

Canadian January out in the garden: the single, bare, elm tree away in the corner, the iced-over patio and barbeque, the drained, snow-filled swimming pool with its rusted stainless steel steps and handrails. Man, is there anything emptier looking than an empty swimming pool?

Without really thinking about it I was searching through my bag and then I was flipping through my address book. I found the number, recently written near the back in a girlish hand, and took the phone down off the wall. Five, six, rings, then a woman's voice—professional, polite—said, "Hello, Gray residence?"

"Uh, hi. Can I speak to Skye, please?"

"May I ask who is calling?"

"It's Greg. Ah, Greg Keltner? I'm a friend of hers."

"One moment please, Mr. Kellner."

There was the sound of the receiver being placed down on a table and footsteps clicking off into the distance, echoing in a big room. I imagined the table, the feet, and the room: seeing in my head lacquered antique wood, an enormous marble hallway, and the polished black flats of the housekeeper, maid, or secretary. A long pause, then faster footsteps were approaching and the scrape of the receiver being picked up. "Hi Greg!" she said, sounding out of breath.

"Hi. You been running or something?"

"Oh, not rilly," she panted. "We were out trying to play tennis, but it's *so* cold. So," her tone changed, getting gentler, kinder, "how did it go? How are you?"

"Oh, OK. It's been OK."

"How's your dad?"

"He's alright. He's sleeping. Listen, when are you guys

heading down?"

"I think we're, well, Jeannie and Warren are coming here and then, OW! *Fuck off* Eric!" she was laughing, like somebody just goosed her or something. "Sorry Greg, err yeah, they're coming here tomorrow and we're gonna head down the day after that. So we'll be there the, uh, the day of the show I guess."

"Right. What you been up to?"

"Just catching up with friends, the usual holiday shit."

"Yeah. Me too. I..." I trailed off, feeling the distance between us, the thousands of miles of snow and ice between here and Vermont. "I'll probably head down tomorrow. Are we all still meeting up in that bar?"

"Yeah, it's near the corner of West 56th and—"

"Broadway. Yeah I know it. I'll see you guys there."

"OK. Are you alright Greg?"

"Yeah, I'm fine. I just...I wanna get back y'know?"

"Fuck yeah. Me too. My family's driving me crazy."

"Yeah, they'll do that," we laughed, but not much. "Well," I said, winding up, "I guess I'll see you in New York."

"Great. Have a good flight."

"Yeah, oh, happy New Year by the way."

"Yeah, same to you Greg."

I hung up. Who the fuck was Eric?

The phone started ringing again. Maybe she'd forgotten something, wanted to ask me something. "Hi."

"Greg?" Jackie. Pissed. Shit. "If you and your father think—"

I just dropped the phone back in the cradle and then took it off the hook. Fuck her. She could stick her sandwiches and her fuckin' coffee up her fuckin' ass. I just wanted to go now, to be back in Woodstock, out on our porch. I wanted it to be summer.

I rang the airline. The earliest flight I could get was tomorrow morning. I took it, but it wasn't enough. "Be here now," I said to myself, like in Alex's book. Alex had been reading this Buddhist book, an Eastern Zen philosophy primer, or some fuckin' thing he'd heard Robbie Robertson talking about one night. He'd leave it lying around the house. According to this book one of the things you had to learn in order to achieve total peace and happiness was that you had to be able to accept, and be serene in, whatever situation, whatever moment, you found yourself in. If you couldn't change the circumstances you had to change your relationship with the circumstances, or something.

I went into the garden and lit a cigarette. A cold wind gusted by, shaking ice and snow from the tree, cutting through me like a pang of yearning, a yearning to be gone. The opposite of homesickness. Be. Here. Now. I said it to myself out loud a second time. "Be here now." Fuck that. "Fuck that," I said out loud, flicking the butt into the empty pool.

Five minutes later I was in the downstairs bathroom with the razor blade, the tightly rolled twenty, and the shaving mirror. Then I was sitting on the edge of the tub with my head tilted back, like I had a nosebleed, saying *"Owwwweee!"* as the speedball stung and dripped sour and burning down the back of my throat. I'd mixed the first line about 70/30 coke/junk and I started feeling the pop, rush, and clarity of the coke with just a tingling, numbing undertow from the junk. I put more of the dirty Chinese heroin in the second line—more than I'd ever done before—making it browner, grittier, sandy-colored—and then I snorted it up through the other nostril in one quick, determined stroke. Man; that did it. The bathroom started to glow and pulse, my vision reddening, and then it was like I was sitting inside a pink, beating heart. I gripped the side of the old cast-iron bathtub, swaying a little, giggling as I rode out a lovely wave of tingling nausea. *"Be here now,"* I chanted softly, lowering myself down into the tub. *"Be. Here. Now."*

* * *

I came round stretched out in the tub.

I don't know how long he'd been sitting there, perched on the can a few feet away, his voice low and his hands busy. Something was flaming, there was fire, orange, near his hands. My vision was swimming as I came up, surfacing out of a beautiful dream. In the dream it was summer and a bunch of us were up at the swimming hole, just outside Woodstock. There was Rick and Richard, Alex, Tommy, Johnny Becker, Howard Alk, Skye, and a few other girls. Even Robbie and Dominique were there. It was summer and I was floating in clear, warm mountain water. You could see all the way down to the bottom. Then something was happening on the bank, some commotion, and I was trying to swim to the shore but I couldn't get there. I was reaching for the bank, strands of grass and weeds coming away in my fingers, and all the while there was shouting and people were running a few feet away. Robbie could see me—could see that I couldn't get out—but he wasn't moving to help me. He just sat there, under a leafy tree, smiling and strumming on his battered old Stella acoustic.

My dad was talking as he worked. The fire was gone and he was doing something with glass and steel now, "And I still see her face. I see it all the time. Her eyes were brown."

"Dad?" I tried to sit up, but, man, I was as weak as a fuckin' kitten.

"Sometimes I can hear her saying to me, very clearly, 'It's alright. I'm OK now. You don't have to worry about me.' Other times..."

"Dad? I..."

"...she'll be angry. She'll shout at me about her life. The life she would have had."

My vision cleared and I saw now that he was carefully resealing my baggie and putting it back in my wash bag. He hefted something up, chrome glinting in the weak late afternoon sunlight that came in through the small, high window, and now I saw the needle, slender as a wasp sting, as a horsehair. A professional's needle: a long-timer's spike. He tied off, the belt between his teeth, the right hand with the loaded, cocked syringe tracking slowly up the left forearm, bringing that fine needle home into the crook of his elbow.

His thumb pushed the plunger home: he clenched his fist briefly, exhaling heavily, his head dropping. He sat like that for a moment, the only sound in the room icy water dripping from the tap in the sink. He wasn't talking about my mom. He was talking about the little girl from the hospital, one of the kids he'd killed; the thing that had sent him down this road and wrecked everything for them. He'd been tired, hungover, jonesing, working a double shift in the emergency room. A bunch of kids who'd been in a big car smash came in and he'd lent too heavily on the morphine and killed three or four of them. I couldn't remember exactly. He hadn't gone to jail; hospital lawyer got him off. My mom kept working and he came home and went into his room with that old hypodermic for the next fifteen years. She got him stuff, pharmaceutical, from the hospital when she could, off the street when she couldn't. I was only seven or eight when it happened, so I couldn't really remember him being anything other than a ghost. Now and again I'd get a flash of him when he was still alive; dancing around the living room with my mom to some goofy old record, showing me places he'd been in the world on the big globe in his study. You can't really remember much before the age of four or five, so I only had three or four years of memories to pick from. There wasn't much. But maybe we still had time to build a few happy moments together.

Feebly I brought my left arm up out of the tub and held it out toward him, wrist side up, veins showing blue through milky skin. My ropes were virginal, in good shape. What would his be like now? Blue cheese. Dust. Rusted plumbing. We looked at each other for a long time before he got up and came and sat on the edge of the tub. He tied me off and tenderly stroked a vein up, the whole scene a crazy parody of a father bathing his child.

"It was a long time ago, Dad."

"No son. Not really."

When I was little I always wanted him to call me "son" more. It was always "Greg" and I melted whenever he called me "son," feeling closer to him. But after a while it was always "Greg" and then, the further he went into himself, he didn't call me anything.

He slipped the needle efficiently, medically, into the thick vein that ran straight into the center of my elbow and pushed her home, shooting me up for the first time.

I saw fireworks in a warm summer sky.

Celluloid burning through in a projector.

White-out.
Black hole.

Eight

"We're gonna put away all of our tears."

The house lights went down and the crowd roared. *"Ohmi-God! Look, it's him!"* a girl behind us squeaked breathlessly. Skye and Jeannie were jumping up and clapping, me and Alex whistling, as Dylan walked out onto the stage at Carnegie Hall, flanked by Robbie and Rick. There were a couple of thousand people packed into the old theater, the air crackling with applause and expectation.

People couldn't believe it, man. He hadn't been on a stage in America in nearly two years—they were all expecting the corkscrew curls, shades, and grinding Telecaster. Not this: short, neat hair, crisp conservative suits in sober dark colors. The Woodstock, *John Wesley Harding* Dylan.

They counted it off and plunged right into Guthrie's "I Ain't Got No Home," taking it hard; Robbie scratching and popping off licks, Dylan scrubbing along' on a big old Martin and Rick—beaming—swaying and hopping around as he pumped out the bass part, his fingers burbling up and down the neck. Richard and Garth had their heads down behind their keyboards either side of the stage. It was the first time we'd really seen Levon playing—he was loving it, man; throwing his head back and looking up into the spotlights as he growled his backing vocals into the mike that hung over his shoulder, his hands flashing around the sparkling drum kit. They were ripping the place up—Rick leaning in to share Dylan's mike, his guitar lead stretching right across the stage, as they both roared out the choruses.

It was great to be back. I'd nearly cried with joy the day before when Manhattan's silver angles suddenly appeared below the plane as we came down; two hundred tons of cold metal falling through the freezing winter cloud and levelling out over the gray scud of the Hudson, my back and limbs stiff in the seat. (I'd woken up in the tub around dawn, my father gone, a ghost that had drifted back off into the upper reaches of the house. I'd wondered—as I rung for a taxi—if I'd dreamt the whole thing. But then I pulled up my sleeve and saw the reddish dot, the bee sting, in the crook of my arm.)

I'd cabbed into the city and gone straight over to Dave's place to reload on some stuff. I stepped over a couple of nodding black kids in the hallway on the way up and rang the bell for a while, muffled noise coming from inside. He answered the door in a full-length fur coat and Cossack hat with a shawl wrapped around him. I whistled. "Wow. What's with the look, man?"

"Fucking heat's on the fritz. Cunt landlord." We headed into the kitchen. Music—well, something in the vicinity of music, something fuckin' insane, metallic sounding—was pounding at incredible volume from Dave's bedroom. There were a few people in there too. It looked like I'd walked in on the tail end of a party that had been going on for a while. Dave was saying something to me.

"What?" I cupped a hand to my ear, trying to drown the noise out.

"YOU WANNA BEER?"

"Yeah, thanks." A neighbor started pounding on a ceiling or a wall somewhere.

"How you been?" he asked me as we walked into the kitchen. There was a girl unconscious on the floor.

"I've been back home. My mom died."

"Shit, man," said Dave, opening the fridge and sounding like I'd just told him I was double-parked. "Ah fuck!" he said, suddenly furious. "Mallory! MALLORY, YOU FUCKING CUNT!" he was screaming at the girl. She was out cold, man. A fucking corpse. Dave picked her head up by the hair, a thin, clear rope of drool connecting her mouth to the dirty linoleum, and screamed in her ear, "WHO DRANK ALL MY HEINEKENS? *WHO DRANK ALL MY FUCKING HEINEKENS YOU FUCKED UP JUNKIE BITCH!*" Nothing. Not a flicker. The music next door was just fucking demented now, bedlam—a blanket of grinding noise and hiss. A guitar cut through it sounding like it was being broken in half. Dave dropped her head and it cracked down off the hard floor. She gave a little moan.

"Sorry, man," Dave said, handing me a can of Bud. "These fucking junkies keep drinking up all my shit."

"Sorry?"

"I SAID—"

"DAVE! TURN THIS FUCKIN' SHIT DOWN MAN!"

"Shhh, man!" he said, putting a finger to his lips and pushing the door shut. "Lou's through there. We've been up for a

couple of days. This is the first pressing of his new record."
Aw shit, not that prick. This was all I fucking needed. "Don't
you like it?" Dave asked, nodding toward the music.

"No, man. It's..." I listened for a second. Now someone
was kicking a drum kit down a flight of stairs while a disem-
bodied voice chanted something over and over. "...It's fucked,
Dave," I laughed.

"Well, you kinda get used to it," he said defensively.

Yeah, like fuckin' herpes. "Listen, sorry Dave, I'm running
late, man. We're going to this Dylan thing at Carnegie Hall
later—"

"Oh yeah, is that tonight? Can you get me in?"

"Ah, maybe. Yeah. I'll...I'll call you later?"

"OK. Thanks, man. Hey Lou, this is Greg," he said as
Reed strolled in. Even with the cold, he was sweating through
his black leather jacket and wraparound shades.

"We've met before. Hi Lou. Sounds great," I said smiling
insincerely, jerking a thumb in the direction of the sound of
blood and torture. He headed for the fridge, didn't reply.

"Greg's going to see Dylan tonight," Dave continued, "at
the Woody Guthrie thing they're having up at Carnegie Hall."

"Yeah?" Lou snarled—already, always, pissed off—"Well
fuck Bob Dylan. Fuck Woody Guthrie. And fuck you." He
pulled out a bottle of something and headed back to the bedroom, back to his awful fuckin' music.

"Sorry, man," said Dave. "He's having a hard time with
John right now."

"Yeah, sure. Can we do this thing?" I asked, yawning, fanning out a roll of fifties.

By the time they were tearing through the last song,
"Grand Coulee Dam," Skye and Jeannie and a couple of the

other girls were up and dancing in the aisles, a lot of people were whooping and hollering. No one was fuckin' booing now, man, although a couple of old folkies nearby us—gray, joyless motherfuckers in their forties—shook their heads at the sight of the girls jumping around to Woody Guthrie songs. This fat old guy caught Alex's eye and said, sadly, "Where's their goddamned couth?" Alex—stoned, still drunk from the Irish bar around the corner before the show—threw his arms around the guy, whooped *"Woo-hooh!,"* kissed him on the cheek, and strutted over toward Skye and the others, shaking his ass. The guy stood wiping his cheek and shaking his head, sad at what had happened to folk music.

After the show we hung around near the stage as the folkies, hippies, hipsters, and all the other losers filed out of the auditorium. After a while Rick and Richard came out and saw us and took us back toward the dressing rooms. There was a girl crying at the door that lead backstage, pleading with one of the security guys—"I have to see Bob Dylan. *I have to*"—Richard put an arm around me as we went through. "How was it?" he asked gently.

"Shit, it was great, man. You really..."

"No, man," he said, "I meant..."

"Oh right. Pretty rough, man. Pretty weird." He squeezed my shoulder.

One big dressing room was packed out with everyone from the show and their entourages. There was Odetta, Pete Seeger, Judy Collins, Arlo Guthrie. I saw Grossman way across the room arguing with some photographer. Man, that guy never stopped. Levon came up, real friendly, "Y'all want a drink?" They had big trash cans filled with ice, beer, sodas, and white wine. You kinda wondered what Woody Guthrie—a man who'd sometimes eaten out of trash cans—would have made of all this. But I didn't wonder too long, I took the cold tube Levon was holding out to me.

"Great show, man."

"Aw hell, it was a bit ragged, but folks seemed to like it. I tell ya son, it made a real nice change from getting booed by a bunch of fucking beatniks! Pardon my French there Miss," he said sweetly to Skye, who laughed at the crazy, old-world courtesy.

A few yards away, Dylan was cornered by a couple of college kids. One of them, a cute teenage chick dressed in all the colors of the rainbow, was asking him questions real sincerely while her friend, a longhaired kid in a poncho and flared lime-green cords, scribbled notes into a pad. Listening to her in his suit and glasses, nodding a little, not making eye contact, Dylan looked like a priest hearing confession. Levon chuckled, "Man, all these kids keep on asking old Bob about his poezisheeun on the war in Vee-et-nam. He starts talking to 'em about old Charlie Joy." Charlie Joy: the carpenter and odd-job man from Woodstock. We laughed.

Another girl, wasted looking in a psychedelic tie-dye wrap, covered in crazy jewelery and with Indian braiding in her hair, came over to where Robbie and Rick were talking and interrupted them, "You guys are in Bob Dylan's band, right?"

"Yeah," Robbie said wearily, for the thousandth time in his life.

"Can I ask you something?" They waited for the question. "Why do you all dress so funny?"

The guys—in their dark suits and shirts—looked at her, this East Village freak show, and just started laughing. What could you say to these fucking people?

Later on we all wound up going to this party on Central Park West, in the Dakota Building. I'd been there once before, delivering grass for Manny to this TV producer fag who'd hit on me. It was in this actor Robert Ryan's apartment— one of those Manhattan places you only see in the movies and on TV: huge, high ceilings, big windows overlooking the park, the whole bit, man. Alex whistled as we came in.

Earlier on in the show Ryan had read from Guthrie's auto-biography and he'd been in that Lee Marvin war movie *The Dirty Dozen* that came out last year. He seemed like a cool old ham. I mean, he must have been seventy years old or some-thing, but he still had that rugged, 1950s leading man charm. Skye was doing her little girl act, saying she wanted to meet him. It was a slightly older, hip crowd and we took over a lit-tle corner and stayed there. I could see Robbie coolly working the room, drink and cigarette in hand. As he drifted over toward us, passing close by, our eyes met and I figured I had to say something. "Hey, great show Robbie."

"Thanks," he nodded.

"Must have been fun playing for people again."

"Yeah, you know..." he trailed off, looking around. I sipped my drink, and then, unexpectedly, he added, "I was sorry to hear about your mom."

"Oh. Thanks. Yeah." I couldn't think of anything else to say. I was always uncomfortable talking to him—those eight words represented about the sum total of unsolicited conver-sation I'd ever had out of the guy—so I just nodded and looked a bit sad. "Hey," I said, remembering how he thought the Velvet Underground were a crock and about to tell him the Lou Reed story, from Dave's apartment yesterday, but somebody called him and he said "Excuse me" and drifted off across the room.

I put my drink down and nudged Richard, "Hey, wanna go to the john and get fucked up?"

"I'm there," he said, draining his glass and putting his hands on my shoulders, "lead on, man." Rick saw what was happening and raised an eyebrow at us. I nodded for him to follow, he nodded to Skye, and the four of us snaked off in a line, heading through the crowd and off down the thickly carpeted hallway. Rick tried a door and found a bedroom. Richard tried another, found the bathroom, and said, "Step into my office."

We came barreling out of there five minutes later, laughing and jumping around, and ran straight into Robert Ryan. "Hello," he said warmly, but obviously not having a fuckin' clue who we were. Rick stuck out his hand, "Mr. Ryan? Rick and Richard, we're in Bob Dylan's band? We met earlier on."

Ryan smiled, "Of course, of course, thanks for stopping by."

Skye butted in. "Mr. Ryan," she simpered, inch-long eyelashes fluttering, "I just wanted to tell you that I thought you were marvellous in the film of Billy Budd. Rilly you were."

"Why thank you dear," Ryan said graciously.

"Yeah, man, and we all fuckin' loved *The Dirty Dozen*," I said, totally straight, gesturing to Rick, Richard, and myself.

"Well," Ryan chuckled self-deprecatingly, looking at us, wondering if we were putting him on, "it keeps a roof over my head. Please excuse me. There's more of the apartment through there if you'd like to have a look." He hurried off along the hall, getting away from these loaded maniacs. We wandered along into another little lounge area. There was a shiny black baby grand piano in there and Richard sat down and played a couple of chords, checking the tuning. Rick, Skye, and I sat on a long sofa, me in the middle between the two of them. "Man," I said, "it must be getting pretty old for you guys, getting called 'Bob's backing band' all the time."

"Well, it won't be for much longer," Rick said. They'd finally signed their deal with Capitol—as the fucking Crackers!—and started work on their own record here in New York a couple of weeks ago. They were going out to LA to finish it at the famous Capitol Records building, the tower place that looked like a bunch of tires all stacked on top of each other.

"You know what songs are gonna be on it?"

"Near enough." Rick said.

"'Bessie Smith'? 'Katie's Been Gone'?"

"Nah, we got some newer stuff, stuff Richard and Robbie have been writing. Maybe a couple of Bob's songs from the basement..." Shit, if they were throwing stuff like that out, what was going on the fuckin' record? "Hey, sing one of yours for Greg, Richard."

"Nah."

He kept doodling on the piano, random notes, little half phrases of melody. But then Skye went off and came back with a bottle of rum she'd swiped and we had a couple more drinks and another line and we talked Richard into singing something. He wouldn't sing one of his own songs—he said he was embarrassed on account of the words not being any good—but he'd do one of Bob's they were going to record. He turned round on the piano stool, in profile to us now, pressed the pedal in, muffling the strings down, and sang a couple of notes, searching for the register, his voice pirouetting up and up toward that trembling falsetto. Then he closed his eyes, softly voiced the chords, sucked in some air, and sang the words:

"They say everything can be replaced..."

Singing them for about the first time outside of a grubby metal and cinder block basement in upstate New York; singing them just for me, Rick, and Skye. It sounded like a hymn. The music drifted over us like absolution, like the little buttons of snow falling past the window, falling down on Central Park in the black January night. When the chorus came up Rick leaned forward, hanging his head down, his eyes closed too, and their voices meshed together: two twenty-four-year-old guys—drinkers, drug-takers, womanizers—sounding older and wiser than they properly had any right to.

"I see my light come shining,
from the west down to the east..,"

A couple of people wandered in from the hall and stood listening. Not many, I mean, it wasn't like Dylan had sat down to play a number—the whole fuckin' place would have stopped—because Rick and Richard weren't famous. They were just a couple of guys in the corner at this show business party, man. You could still hear the hubbub coming from the other side of the apartment, all the normal conversation and drinking going on while this amazing thing was happening a few feet away from us.

Richard let the last chord fade away and juiced the final few drops of emotion out of the last line:

"I shall be released..."

Hearing this song, with everything that had happened in the past few weeks, was like being punched in the stomach and it seemed strange that it was all over—this perfect, incredible thing—in less time than it takes to boil an egg, smoke a cigarette, or fill up your car.

He took his hands off the keys and swivelled back around to face us, shrugging. There was a silence for a couple of seconds then everyone—me, Ricky, Skye, the couple in the doorway—started clapping. Richard mumbled something self-deprecating, lit a fresh cigarette (and I noticed now that, true to form, he'd left the last one burning on the edge of Robert Ryan's expensive-looking, pristine piano), and nodded sheepishly at the little round of applause. I turned around to say something to Skye and saw that she was slipping out of the room, looking like she was trying not to run.

The guy from the doorway came over and introduced himself, shook Richard's hand, and started asking him stuff about music. Rick turned to me smiling and said, "The guy can fucking sing, you know?"

"Yeah," I said quietly, still numb, like I'd just been emptied, cleaned out by the song. "The guy can fucking sing."

Nine

"Hear the sound, Willie Boy..."

A week or so after the Carnegie Hall show I was heading down to the city to make a couple of pick ups when Richard called, asking if I had any speed. They were working late nights in the studio and he wanted to keep sharp.

We arranged to meet on the corner of Seventh and West 54th. I came up out of the subway, screwing my eyes up against sunshine: one of those late winter days in New York City where you get July sun and January cold at the same time, the whole town fresh and clean and shining real hard. I was running late, jogging and weaving through the midtown bustle, the sidewalk full of lunchtime people—the secretaries and Mr. Joneses hurrying out with their dry cleaning and back with their deli-wrapped sandwiches—when I saw Richard leaning against a phone booth in front of Carnegie's. He was wearing shades, brown-bagging, and reading a newspaper like he hadn't a care in the fuckin' world, oblivious to all these pissed-off looking people swarming around him, scowling at him for having the brass balls to look like he didn't give a shit about them and their world of charts and customers and the E train home at five o'clock. Shit, tell me Richard Manuel didn't look fuckin' cool leaning there amongst all the regular people, reading his paper and drinking his brew.

"Hey, man," I said, popping out of the crowd, surprising him, "how you doing?" We embraced warmly—attracting a few more stares—and he took his sunglasses off. He looked tired. "So how's the record going?" I asked.

"Great, man. You wanna come up and hear something?"

I'd never been in a recording studio before. But I didn't really want to walk into some tiny little sound booth with Robertson, Grossman, and whoever all staring at me. "Ah, I don't know. Maybe—"

"Hey, it's cool. There's only me, John, and Garth up there right now."

The place—A&R studios it was called—was only a couple of blocks away. We rode up in an old elevator, the kind that smells of oil and warm valves, with creaky metal gates. Somewhere above us, echoing down the dusty shaft, I could hear something like fairground music swirling in the distance. I handed Richard a paper bindle with about thirty of those little pink amphetamine pills he loved so much wrapped tightly inside. "Great," he said, pulling a huge crumpled wad of bills from his jeans, trying to juggle the money, the wrap, and his drink at the same time, dropping tens and twenties all over the place, "what do I owe you?"

"Don't worry about it. Just gimme a copy of the record when it's done, OK?"

"Shit Greg, you'll get that anyway. Thanks..." I bent down, picked up the sixty odd bucks he'd missed—the fairground music getting much louder, closer to us, now—and stuffed the bills into his shirt pocket.

"Be careful with all that dough in the city, man." You often wound up feeling like Richard's mom, even me.

"Hell, its only money."

The elevator spasmed to a halt and we stepped out into this huge dark room: like an enormous barn, with fluorescent tubes humming in the ceiling high above us. The organ music was deafening now and I could see Garth across the room, hunched behind the organ, producing this incredible sound, the whole maelstrom booming deafeningly around the giant empty space, Garth's head swaying back and forth, eyes closed, lost somewhere in the middle of this thing he was creating. It sounded like five people playing a couple of instruments each.

Levon's Gretsch drum kit was set up in the middle of the room, surrounded by screens, I guess to help block off some of the noise. The cymbals were shimmering and fizzing as they gently vibrated in the wash of noise Garth was making. A couple of Fender amps, stacks, faced each other in front of the kit, Robbie's Telecaster propped up against one. I followed Richard over to a corner where there was an enormous grand piano, the signs of a recent and lengthy occupation by Richard were scattered all around it; cigarette packets, paper cups, cans and bottles, sheets of lyrics and music, ashtrays. He sat down on the piano bench and washed two of the pills I'd given him down with a couple of inches of cold black coffee, grimacing and shaking his head, chasing them down his throat. Garth suddenly stopped playing—the silence immediate and total—and padded around in his shoeless feet to a couple of big speaker cabinets, humming a little tune to himself and giving us a wave as he went. "You look tired, man," I said to Richard.

"Yeah, we've been working late most nights. I..." he trailed off, looking up at the strip lighting, a single white bar reflecting in each of his dark eyes, "...it's funny. I miss Jane, y'know?" I hadn't met Jane, Richard's ex-girlfriend, his sweetheart, but he talked about her sometimes when he was drunk and lonely. Rick told me she was a knockout, a teenage Swedish model or something, when they met her in Toronto a few years back. Her and Richard had only been together for a few months before Bob Dylan rolled into the Hawks' lives and took them off around the world, changing everything, but you could tell he'd really fallen for her in that time.

"Yeah? Is she seeing anyone now?"

He shook his head. "I don't think so. She was engaged to some guy, but she broke it off."

"Why don't you give her a call, man?"

"We talk on the phone here and there but, I don't know, with all this going on..." he gestured around the room at the amps, speakers, and wires, "...and we'll probably be back on the road again when the record's out. It ain't no kind of home life. I don't know if it would work. Y'know? Could we keep it together?"

"Well, only one way to find out."

"Yeah..." He plinked a couple of high notes on the piano, stared off across the big room. I didn't really understand how a guy like Richard—a happening musician, record deal, making an album, good-looking—could get as lonely as he got sometimes. "Hey," he said, getting up, "come on through and hear some music."

We went through a couple of thick doors and came into

a smaller room full of dials, meters, switches, and buttons. There was a little guy, pleasant looking, about our age, sitting at the mixing console. I recognized him from one night at Deanie's. "Hey John," Richard said, slapping him on the shoulder. "This is Greg, a good friend of ours from Woodstock."

"Pleased to meet you Greg," he said, real nice and polite, offering his hand.

"Hi," I shook it and we sat down in some chairs behind him. A burst of organ notes came clear and strong through the speakers mounted in front of us, then Garth's voice, echoing, distant, "Is that better John?"

"That's much better, thank you Garth. OK, come on through and we'll hear some back." He pressed another button, moved some faders, and Garth's organ filled the tiny room as the man himself came through the door. I got up and offered him my seat but he just smiled and motioned for me to sit back down. He bowed his head and listened with his eyes closed as John turned the volume up. I'd never heard anything like it in my life; it sounded like a fairground, a classical music concert, a horror film soundtrack, and a whirlwind all being blasted through the PA at a rock concert at the same time. It went on for maybe half a minute, building and building, getting more intricate and insane as Garth added notes and textures, bent pitch, and shaped sound. I turned and looked up at its creator, who was standing beside me listening, smiling, and tapping a little screwdriver against his teeth. With his huge, crackling beard, high forehead, and tweedy jacket Garth looked like a cross between General Grant and a professor of archaeology at some Ivy League university. Finally, when the swell of organ just couldn't build anymore, drums and a gutsy guitar riff kicked in and the whole thing coalesced into one almighty groove.

"Holy shit!" I said, unable to be cool. "How do you do that, man?"

Garth smiled. "Well, I had a little help from Johann Sebastian." He padded off back through to the studio.

"John Sebastian—The Lovin' Spoonful's John Sebastian?" I asked, confused.

"*Johann* Sebastian," said John. "Bach. The initial progression is kind of a riff on Bach's Toccata and Fugue in D minor. But then Garth goes off into his own thing..."

"These rock and roll kids, they don't know nothing John," Richard said, laughing, as John faded the music up higher, vocals coming in now, and I put my head down, closed my eyes, and just went with it.

* * *

They really started arriving that spring, the spring of '68.

By April the long, steely mountain winter had finally begun to let go—shoots, buds, leaves, and the windows thrown open on houses—and they started coming up from the city in Camaros, Pintos, and Beetles; their bedding, guitars, record collections, and potted plants crammed into the trunks and backseats. They came across the country in VW vans and station wagons. Walking down Tinker Street you started noticing the license plates—Wisconsin, California, Florida, Washington.

On the weekend it started to get harder to get a good table at Deanie's or the Café Espresso and, if you cocked your ear and tuned into some of the conversations going on around the room in those places, you didn't have to wait too long before you heard somebody saying the words "Bob Dylan." They all wore the new uniforms: tie-dye, loon pants, kaftans, bells, beads, and tinted sunglasses. We didn't look like that, me and Alex and Tommy and the guys in the Hawks. We dressed more like the locals: black clothes, check shirts, tighter pants, shorter hair. We looked like fuckin' undertakers in this sea of colorful longhairs.

While all of this could be a major pain in the ass when you were trying to eat, or get a beer, I had to admit that, as far as business was concerned, the newcomers were good news for me. So-and-so would talk to such-and-such who would mention that they'd gotten whatever from what's-his-name and, soon enough, our phone would be ringing and there'd be some cheerful hippie girl, some nervous college boy, on the line asking me if I could "turn them on, man."

After a while I had Alex and Johnny B doing odd runs for me, taking deliveries over to Bearsville and Saugerties, dropping stuff off at the wood frame houses set back in the woods off the roads through the mountains. We were becoming a regular cottage industry and the green was starting to tumble in—I had a shoebox with six thousand dollars in it hidden beneath a false bottom in my wardrobe—some serious fuckin' money at that time, man. I bought myself a black '65 Corvette Stingray, the last year of the fuel-injected Stingrays—Levon loved that car and got himself a gold one a little while later—and my first real nice guitar, a beautiful old 1938 Martin 0017, one of the little-bodied ones. Dylan had one just like it.

The only real downside to all this was that I was starting to find myself hitting the Thruway down to New York every Thursday and coming back up with the glove box bursting with uppers, downers, speed, coke, junk, and four or five different kinds of weed. I tried to talk Dave into getting bigger deliveries so I could cut the number of trips I had to make back down to once or twice a month, but he was jittery about having those kinds of amounts in the house and—the way Dave lived—I didn't blame him. So I started using the black guys on Tenth Avenue more regularly for the heavier stuff. They stepped on it more but they always had it.

It was late afternoon and we were out on the porch for the first time that year—Alex, this girl Susie he was seeing, and little Tommy and me—drinking beer and passing around a strong stick of Thai weed. The living room windows were open, the first Buffalo Springfield album coming out of them. The sun was sinking down into the tree line now and green was starting to come back into the woods. It had rained earlier, a clean April shower, and in the scratchy seconds between tracks you could hear rainwater dripping from the guttering and the pines around the house, ticking from the wet branches, plopping into the water barrel next to the porch.

From somewhere along Ohayo Mountain Road came the sound of a car engine, dropping as it took the corner near our turn off, then revving hard again as it got closer, screeching as it came around the bends too fast. Alex looked at me, smiled, and said "that asshole." The engine grew louder and I shook my head as my Corvette appeared through the trees, coming fast up the single track road, Johnny B at the wheel. He hit the brakes hard and spun the wheel at the same time, throwing the car around in a skidding semicircle in front of the house, wet gravel and mud slurring from under the fat radials. He got out grinning and came bounding up the steps, arms raised in triumph. "And once again, Juan Manuel Fangio takes the checkered flag! Hi Alex, hey baby..." he ruffled Susie's hair.

"I've told you to stop driving my car like that you fuckin' asshole."

"Relax, man, I've done your bidding." He threw his scarf around his neck and dropped a tightly banded roll of bills into my lap. "Hey douchebag, good timing," he said, snatching the beer Tommy had just popped open out of his hand and guzzling it down.

"Hey! Fuck you, man!" Tommy protested. "Get your own fucking beer Johnny!" Johnny kept guzzling like he was going to drink the whole thing. "I mean it, you fucker! Don't finish my beer! Do. Not. Drink. My. Beer."

I flipped through the money. "Hey, shouldn't there be more than this?"

"If you...if you finish that fucking beer, Johnny."

Johnny finished the beer and scrunched the can up, letting rip a huge belch at the same time.

"You fucker," Tommy said, trudging off to the kitchen to get another.

"Yeah, there should be," Johnny said, taking Tommy's chair, lighting a cigarette, "but you know that guy, the guy over on Spencer Road...the guy with the hair and stuff? Donnie is it?"

"Donnie with the green Camaro?" Alex said.

"That's the fucker."

"Yeah?" I said.

"He only had half the money. He said he'd give it to you in Deanie's tomorrow night. Said you'd be OK with that." He picked up my Martin and sounded a bright chord. "You're OK with that, aren't you, man? He's a good guy."

"I guess. Asshole should have called me. You should have called me."

"Yeah, what you gonna do? Goddamn potheads are so unreliable." He looked out at the trees and the setting sun. "Nice evening though, ain't it?"

"It sure is," said Susie. Tommy came back with his fresh beer.

"Hey, thanks Tee," Johnny joked, reaching out to take it.

"Fuck you, I was sitting there too Johnny!"

"Hey," Johnny said turning back to me, ignoring Tommy, "I just saw your girlfriend in Café Espresso. What's-her-name...Skye?"

"Yeah, he wishes," said Alex. Skye hadn't been around much in the past couple of months; she'd written me once, saying that she was going to have to put some work in this semester or they were going to kick her out of Columbia. I hadn't expected her to be up here now though because Rick wasn't around—The Hawks/The Crackers/The Honkies/whatever (they'd been trying out a new name every other week recently) were all still down in California. "Skye Gray?" said Susie. "The girl from Vermont? She is so pretty."

"Tell us something we don't know baby," said Johnny. "Anyway, where you deadbeats want to eat tonight?"

"I got a feeling we might just be heading over to Café Espresso," Alex said, smiling at me.

"Fuck you, she's just a friend," I said, getting up. Alex and Johnny laughed. As I walked off Johnny started playing "My Girl," Alex singing along too—*"What can make me feel this way..."*—drowning out Steven Stills coming from the stereo as I headed upstairs through the darkening house to change my shirt.

When we came in I did that looking-around-the-room-then-being-surprised-to-see-you-thing: doing a double take when I saw her waving at us, Johnny and Alex snickering as they went to the bar. She was with Jeannie, Grace, and some of those other New York chicks and she had on a tight black turtleneck and her hair was up in a turquoise headscarf/bandana thing. I went on over and joined them, Skye patting the chair next to her for me to sit down. She was eating fried chicken, her perfect teeth tearing meat off the bone, her fingers getting greasy and slippery while she talked and laughed. I ordered some too. She looked like she'd gotten some sun. "You look like you've gotten some sun," I said.

"Oh, didn't I say? I went out to LA for a few days. My dad had to go down on business." Man, what about all this *"They're kicking me out of school"* bullshit?

"Yeah? Did you see the guys?"

"They were in the same hotel! The Marmont? On Sunset?" I'd never been to LA, hadn't been much further south than New Jersey, but I nodded anyway. "We'd just checked in and Levon came up and made like he was gonna throw me in the pool! Christ, my dad thought he looked like a wild man!"

Fuckin' rich girl. Rocking around the place on Daddy's fuckin' dime. "Do you want another drink?" I said.

We all got drunk and went on to Deanie's. People were dancing. "Dock of the Bay" come on and Skye pulled me up on the floor, swaying against me, her head resting on my chest and her right hand folded into my left, real dainty, as we did a corny little waltz.

"I left my home in Georgia..."

Cropper's guitar part came glinting through the smoky air like a beam of light, nudging Otis's voice along, nudging it on for the last time. He was dead 48 hours after they recorded this. The tiny airplane, barreling down through Wisconsin sky toward the lake with Otis and the guys from that soul band (the Bar-Kays?) all screaming and praying. Man, was that a hard, shitty break. Shit, was that only last December? It felt like years ago.

"Cause I've had nothing to live for..."

I kept my back to Alex and the others and got as close as I could to her hair without blowing it. She smelled of apples, chestnuts, and cigarettes. She was humming along with the record and I could feel her voice vibrating against my heart, her breasts resting on my rib cage. "I meant to ask you," I said to the top of her head. "How come you took off that night?"

"What night?"

"At that party after the Dylan show, after Richard was singing?"

"Oh, that. I wasn't feeling too good," she was talking into my chest and I had to bend into her to hear, the smell of her hair getting stronger, tearing me up. "Too much grass."

"Looks like nothing's gonna change."

We held each other and went on swaying around in a little semicircle. Then she lifted her head and looked up at me, bourbon sweet on her breath, and said sadly, "People think of this as kind of a happy song, don't they?"

"Yeah, I guess they do."

"But the verses are so sad."

"Maybe you just think that because he died."

"No, they just are."

"And this loneliness won't leave me alone."

"Maybe it's because he whistles at the end," I said as the song faded out and the barman announced last call. "It doesn't leave you feeling sad."

"Maybe," Skye said, smiling now, her arms around my neck, "you got anything nice at home? I feel like staying up a while."

"The doctor is in," I said, leading her back to the table as "All Along the Watchtower" came on.

We were still up after everyone else had gone to bed, smoking the last of my Thai stick and running through the whiskey. It was still cold enough to have a fire going at night and Alex had managed to light one when we came back in. The last few logs of our last cord of wood bitched and spat in the grate, throwing shapes—leaping dogs and trembling monsters—on the walls. The fire and the white strip under the kitchen doorway were the only lights in the room.

We were lying on opposite ends of the sofa, passing the joint back and forth. Strangely we had no music playing. We were just listening to the Catskills wind blowing hard by outside, making the old wooden house ache and groan. We were talking about the guys in the band. "So," I said, sipping Canadian Club, trying to sound casual, "how's it been going with Rick?"

"Rick? He's funny. He cracks me up. He's such a..." she thought for a moment, "he thinks he's such a hustler, Mr. Businessman thing. Not like Robbie. Now there's the real deal."

"How do you mean?"

"He's just business. I don't really think he'd care if most people lived or died as long as he gets where he's going."

"Where's that?"

"The big time I guess." She passed the jay back and asked me. "Do you think their record's gonna be good?"

I nodded slowly, taking a long toke and said, "Don't you?"

"Yeah, but what do I know? I thought the International Submarine Band was gonna be bigger than the Rolling Stones." We laughed. "I had such a crush on Gram a couple of years back."

"What's he like?"

"Rilly nice. I haven't seen him since he joined the Byrds, but he was nice back then. He comes from money so he doesn't feel like he has to try too hard to impress people."

"Did you ever..." Man, I was like a guy with a sore tooth. Just couldn't leave it alone.

"With Gram? No. *Nearly* one time. But we were both so wasted. I had such a crush on him for a while though..."

"And now Rick, hey, you're getting through 'em baby!" I said brightly, jokily, but inside I was feeling anything but. I was feeling like lead. There was a pain in my throat, like I'd swallowed a piece of glass. I gulped some whiskey and reached down and picked up my Martin, just to have something to do with my hands, wanting to feel reassurance in its lacquered spruce and rosewood, its curves put together before the war, before I was born. I played a few soft notes, just popping them off randomly, without reason or melody.

"Rick's fun," she said after a while. "But it's never going to go anywhere."

Right away, the lead melting, turning into sunshine and air, my heart doing flip flops as I fretted a shaky chord and asked her, as casual as I could, "How come?"

She looked right at me, orange spots of fire reflecting in her green eyes and said, "Because I'm in love with someone else."

I stopped playing. A log crumpled to dust as it slithered over in the fire and died. The wind slapped the shingles and rattled the walls. "I have been for months now..." she said, looking down now, unsure whether to go on or not.

Our feet were inches apart—almost touching—and I sat forward too, my guts all trying to move around and rearrange themselves; trying to fit into different places, the wrong, the right, places. In the firelight she looked like a goddamn painting. Should I just kiss her now? No. Let her get this out. It had been building for a while.

"Greg, I..." Her bottom lip trembled as she searched for the words, I opened my mouth, to tell her it was OK, that I felt the same way, but she finished her sentence first. "I'm in love with Richard."

* * *

A few things happened at once: I gulped down three fingers of whiskey, Skye started crying, I moved toward her, to comfort her I guess, and suddenly it all hit me together: the booze, the fried chicken, the Thai Stick, the force of what she'd just said. I bolted down the hall to the bathroom and threw up everywhere.

I was in there for a while. When I came back she was gone; the cold wind coming in through the open kitchen door and a note on the table, held down by a half-empty wine bottle. The bottom of the bottle was wet and the red wine had made a semicircle, a crescent, around the corner of the paper, like a seal. In her elegant, classy handwriting it said:

> *Please don't tell anyone.*
> *Esp Richard.*
> *I'll see you soon,*
> *S. xxx*

Ten

"Your heart's gonna give right out on you..."

It was dusk, the Sunday after Easter, and I was driving along Ohayo Mountain Road, heading home from the pink house.

I'd heard they'd just got back from California, from finishing up their record, and I'd swung by to say hi only to find they were in the middle of packing the last of their stuff up. "Gimme a hand with this sumbitch," Levon had said, coming down around the house with a box full of wires and mikes and shit. I helped him put it in the trunk of Rick's car. There was another box already in there: it was full to the brim with boxes and reels of quarter-inch tape, dozens of them. The box on top had the word "Bob" written on it on red pen. "Anything good here?" I asked, handing him the freshly rolled jay I'd taken from behind my ear. "Ah, here and there we might have landed on something," he drawled, sitting down on the fender and lighting it up, "mostly there." He grinned, a purple cloud of smoke spreading all around him, sweet-smelling in the wet, woody air.

"How was LA?"

"It was good, man. Great studio. I tell you something though, you ever have something called sushi?"

"Have what?"

"Sue-shee."

"Is it dope?" I frowned at the thought of this strange new drug.

He laughed. "No, man, fish. Raw goddamned fish!"

I made a face.

"I know! That's what I figured, but—ah swear—that is some dee-licious shit right there. Me and John wound up eating it every day." We walked up to the house, laughing. "Every fucking day!" Levon repeated, like he could hardly believe it.

Their lease was up and, besides, the place was too small now for Richard, Rick, Garth, and whoever else was always around. Rick and Levon were moving over toward Bearsville. Richard and Garth—real Odd Couple shit there—had found a place to rent right along the road from us. I looked into the living room; bags and boxes all over the floor, the shelves bare, all the little curios and odds and ends had been packed away, the glowing beer sign had been taken down from over the fireplace. A lot of instruments—guitars, a fiddle, an accordion—were packed up near the door, ready to go. The room was doing that thing places do when they empty out and go from being homes back to being just houses again: it seemed bigger and smaller at the same time and the walls were yellowed from the tens of thousands of cigarettes that had been smoked in here in the past year.

I hadn't seen any of them in a few weeks. It was especially strange seeing Richard after what Skye had said. I was looking at him in this whole other light, her love conferring new powers on him, casting him in different, stronger, colors.

Richard sang with something going on in his throat—maybe in his heart—like what I'd felt a few days before, when I thought she was going to finish that sentence with "you" rather than with "Richard." It was something he could call on when he sang the kind of songs that talked about the way I felt afterward, about how I felt when she said his name, not mine. I didn't tell him what Skye had said. I wouldn't be doing that. I went to the basement before I left to carry a couple of guitars out for them. It was empty now. Just cinder block walls, an old boiler, and a few cigarette butts on the cement floor.

The car coming toward me started flashing its lights, slowing down. It was Alex. I stopped in the middle of the road and he pulled up beside me. Susie was sitting in the passenger seat. She was crying. "What's happened, man?" I asked him.

"Shit, ain't you heard?"

"Heard what?"

"King." He shook his head slowly. "They killed King."
We went home and turned on the news and people gradually arrived round at our place. Jeannie and Susie were crying and comforting each other. They were both New Yorkers, both their parents were active in civil rights, the NAACP and stuff like that—then little Tommy, looking lost and sad, like he'd didn't understand what the fuck was happening. Johnny B walked in the door with a quart of rum, and said, "Niggers ain't gonna take this," knowing how the girls would react. "Shut the fuck up, Johnny!" Susie said.

Sure enough, the whole country was going fuckin' crazy, man. Chicago, Memphis, LA. Goddamn places were burning to the ground. Then you walked away from the TV and looked out over your porch. All you'd see was trees and sky.

All you'd hear was maybe a buzzsaw going, somebody cutting themselves a cord of wood. The whole thing seemed unreal. More people arrived—Rick, Richard—and we all got loaded, the night gradually turning from a wake into a kind of half-assed party.

* * *

I was in the kitchen with the back door open, sitting at the table in a warm square of sunlight with my Martin, a sheet of paper, and a pencil. I was trying to write a song; I had a melody in my head and the first line, "*She left unexpectedly...*" which I thought was good. Kinda Beatlesy, to start a story suddenly like that, you know? Like people are gonna be thinking, Who is she? Why did she leave? Where's she going, man? I scribbled those words and a couple of chords down and strummed randomly, searching for a rhyme for "unexpectedly." See? Da dah dee, something "be"? I could hear Alex upstairs, wandering around getting dressed. He had the Doors on, Jim Morrison screeching his thing. It was one of those freak summer days you sometimes got in the springtime, when it wasn't just "nice" weather. It was real nice. Something "see"? "Be"? Too obvious. What would Dylan do? Bring a character's name in? Maybe something biblical? Mary? Didn't quite rhyme, but if you sang it "*May-ree.*"

Mary...Mary...sweet Mary mother of God writing songs was fuckin' hard. I'd been tying to write this goddamned thing for a month now.

I relit the joint and tried to think about biblical images. I remembered looking at that stained glass window in the little chapel at my mom's funeral. Then I remembered not really feeling anything one way or another about it. That was no good; you had to be feeling some way or other about something in a fuckin' song. What was I feeling? From upstairs— *"Father? Yes, son? I want to kill you."* Alex turned it up. I closed the door. What was I feeling more than anything right now?

I want to fuck Skye and have her tell me that she loves me. "Fuck Me and Tell Me That You Love Me." It wasn't Dylan, man.

Skye, she was so fuckin' contrary. She'd call sometimes and we'd talk for a while about this and that, whatever bullshit. She hadn't been to class for a few days the other week; some anti-war protestors—the kind of kids you saw wandering along Camelot Road, looking for Dylan's place, wanting to wave notebooks and cameras at him and ask him what the fuck he was gonna do about Vietnam—had bust into the Columbia offices and taken over the college. They'd called in the cops to get 'em out and Skye said the cops had thrown a good beating on some of them. She'd say she'd be doing this and then you'd hear from someone else that she'd done that. She'd say she didn't think it'd go anywhere with Rick and then she'd be down here weekends and you'd see them coming down Tinker Street. Contrary.

Unexpectedly. Fuck, man. That rhymed, or near enough. I hadn't heard the word "contrary" in a song. It was a cool word. *"She left unexpectedly, she was always so contrary."* I wrote it down quickly.

Fired up, I started strumming the couple of chords I had so far and sang the words, trying to make 'em fit the chord change, and searching for something else, someplace to take it from here. Someone rapped sharply at the screen door. I jumped a little and looked up; Richard was grinning sheepishly through the tattered old mesh. "Shit, you scared me!" I said, a little embarrassed in case he'd been there a while. "Come on in."

"Sorry, man." He was wearing summer stuff—sunglasses, check shorts, striped top, and sandals—and carrying a plastic bag. "What you up to?"

"I was just fucking around," I said, putting the guitar down quickly. "You want some coffee or something?"

"You got a beer? Hot out there today."

He sat down at the table and I got him a Rolling Rock from the fridge. Out the corner of my eye I saw him looking at the sheet of paper. "You writing a song?"

"Shit, I'm trying to."

"You got a tune?"

"Kind of."

"I get tunes all the time. Words—that's a whole other thing. That's fuckin' hard."

"You ain't kidding," I said, handing him the beer. I'd opened one for myself instinctively, even though it was only, like, eleven a.m.

"Bob," Richard said, taking a sip, "he'll get up in the morning, sit down at that typewriter, and write three fuckin' songs before he eats lunch."

"Shit." We both shook our heads. "It's taken me a month to get two fuckin' lines," I said, pulling the sheet of paper toward me, guilty, embarrassed.

"Yeah, I'm the same, man. It comes a little easier to Robbie." We drank our beer in the sunny kitchen. "So," he grinned, "you gonna play it for me?"

"Fuck no. I'm not much of a singer."

"Come on, play me what you got."

"No way."

"You know, I got a little bit of music that might fit with this."

"Yeah?" Shit, he was offering to help me with my fuckin' song.

He picked up the guitar and tweaked the tuning some, then he sounded this little chord progression through a couple of times, humming to himself, cleared his throat, and sang the words I'd just written down, "*She left unexpectedly,*" Jesus Christ. It was like something else altogether: where I'd just had two chords to cover the whole thing, Richard stretched his melody across something like five—C, E, A minor, somthing I didn't get it all—in the space of one line, wringing the words "unexpectedly" and "contrary" out for a long time, the changes from major to minor making it sound bittersweet, up and down, making my version sound just sad and flat. He stopped. "Something like that."

"Yeah, that could work," I said, nodding, as Alex padded in, yawning, bare-chested. "Hi Richard. How's it going?"

"Good, man. What you guys doing today?"

"Going up to the swimming hole, you wanna come?"

"Nah, Bill's driving me to the airport."

"Where you headed?" I asked.

"Back to Stratford. My brother's getting married. I'm gonna take Jane to the wedding."

"Yeah? Are you guys..."

"We'll see," he smiled shyly. "Shit, I gotta run. You want me to write those chords down for you?"

"Are you sure? Don't you wanna use them?"

"Nah, it's cool. I got enough music. Maybe you can help me with some words sometime?" He scribbled the chords down in his shaky handwriting and got up to leave. "Oh, I nearly forgot, the whole reason I came over." He went into his bag and handed me a record. It was heavy—way heavier than normal—with a blank white label in a plain paper sleeve. "That's for you."

"What is it?"

"It's our record, man. Test pressing." I looked at it.

"Wow," Alex said.

"Shit Richard, don't you want to keep this?"

"It's OK, we got a few. Let me know what you think. I gotta run. See you later." He skipped on out the door into the sunshine, humming his version of my song as he disappeared around the corner of the house.

I took the heavy slab out and held it up carefully by the edges. We stared at it; at our faces reflected in a black, glistening pool. There wasn't a mark on it. It'd never been played. "Well," Alex said after a moment, "what are you waiting for?"

* * *

Over an hour later—Alex hung sideways on the armchair, me propped on some pillows on the rug in front of the big speakers—and we were on our second straight listen. The first time through, from the moment Richard sang the first line—"*We carried you, in our arms*"—until he sang the last one—"*I shall be released*"—the song he'd sung that night in Robert Ryan's apartment—neither us had said a word. The only time one of us had moved was when I got up to turn it over, after the song that went "*Take a load off Fannie...*"— the one everybody would be singing soon. (We figured it was probably one of the tunes Dylan had given them.) When the record finished we'd just looked at each other for a second before I turned it right over and put it on again.

When Richard walked out the kitchen door earlier, he'd just been Richard: funny, nervy, shy, sad, kind Richard. Now I knew, I really *knew*, that Richard—and Rick and Levon, Robbie, and Garth—they were a different order of human being from me. It made me feel about twelve years old, made me feel like I knew nothing about music, like I'd never held a guitar in my life. We didn't have any track listing or credits or anything, so you didn't know who'd written what, but Richard sang one I was sure must be his, a soft, dreamy ballad that had the lines:

> *"Once I climbed up the face of a mountain,*
> *and ate the wild fruit there."*

Right away it made me think about the times the summer before; when we sat out back at the pink house, speeding, tripping, drinking, and watching the sun come up on Overlook Mountain. Sitting here in front of the speakers, it seemed like all I'd gotten out of those nights were some bad hangovers and maybe a few bucks. Somehow Richard had gotten this song: this incredible fuckin' thing that might be around forever. The actual sound of the thing too...it was liquid and funky, it sounded brand new—like nothing I'd ever heard before—and, at the same time, it sounded *ancient*: older than the flaking timbers and rusted scraps of West Hurley that swirled on the bottom of the Ashokan. Richard's voice was hard to listen to on some tracks, the way it was recorded, pushed way up so it sat right on top of everything, raw and exposed. It was nearly too much.

After the second time through Alex got up and stretched. "Wow," he said, "that's really something, huh?" I didn't say anything. I still couldn't speak. He picked up a towel from the back of the couch. "Come on, we're missing the rays."

"You go ahead, man. I just wanna listen to this again." He looked at me like I was a little nuts, scooped his car keys out of the wooden bowl on the coffee table, and left.

Looking down, I was surprised to see I still had an unlit joint in my left fist. I torched it up, took a huge, lung-scorching toke, turned the heavy record over for the third time, and cranked the volume about as far as it would go without distorting. There was crackle, silence, then Robbie's guitar, phased, strange sounding, the groove slower than a math class, warm as heroin. There was a line in the first song I wanted to hear again, a line that had been getting closer and closer to me with every listen: "*What dear daughter...could treat a father so.*" I realized that it was a parent talking, singing about being betrayed, let down in some way by their kids. It was a crock, the whole Jim Morrison "Fuck you Mom and Dad" thing. People brought you here out of some kind of love and then it all turned to shit for them and you hated them for it. It was no more their fault than someone not being able to finish a song they were trying to write. I thought about calling my mom and telling her that I was sorry, that it wasn't her fault my dad was a junkie, that I didn't know who I'd been mad at. But I couldn't do that now, because she wasn't at the end of a phone anymore. She was powder and tiny pieces of carbonized bone in a silver tub on a shelf down in the basement back home.

I fucking lost it, man, not just a little bit either. I curled up in a ball on the rug and cried hard as my friend Richard sang the words "*Tears of rage, tears of grief...*" over and over.

When I woke up it was just getting dark out. The windows were still open, mountain air blowing gently in. From where I was laid out I could see the moon and right away I had a line from the record in my head: *"Fell asleep until the moonlight woke me, and I could taste your hair."* There was a hissing, bumping noise, the needle still trundling in the run-out groove. I rubbed my eyes and my knuckles came away wet and salty.

I got up and went through to the kitchen. The scrap of paper with my words and Richard's chords scribbled on it was still on the table. I picked it up and looked at it. Yeah, I was about right: C—E 7th—A min—F.

I tore my song into two, four, eight pieces and dropped them in the trash.

* * *

It was hot by May, and maybe spring felt like summer because the winter seemed to have lasted so long. The sun poured down on the town and a fuming heat-haze rippled up from the roads and sidewalks. People were quickly into shirtsleeves and summer dresses and were eating ice cream, drinking cold sodas, and reading the Sunday newspapers on the green and in the cafés. Cars rolled by kicking up yellow balls of dust, the windows down and music blaring out. Alex and I were walking to the car, going grocery shopping, when Rick's big Continental pulled up alongside us and he got out. He looked cool, a black Fedora hat pulled down against the sun. "Hey Greg," he said. He had a new girlfriend now, this chick Grace, and we weren't seeing so much of them since they moved out of the pink house.

"Hi, man. How's it going?"

"Good. You heard the news?"

"No."

"About Richard?" He was already laughing, shaking his head.

"Shit, what?" What now? Another car smash? A broken limb? Valium overdose?

"About his wedding?" Rick said.

"You mean his brother's wedding?"

"No, man. *His* wedding. He goes to his brother's wedding, he takes Jane with him, and then *they* go and get married!"

"Richard and Jane got married?"

"Yeah! He's hardly seen her in two years, he goes back to Canada for a week and fucking marries her!"

It was crazy, impulsive. Pure Richard.

Eleven

"I believe I know what we should do..."

We sat there, not saying anything. I watched a drop of beer trickle down the side of my frosted glass for a long, long time. It ran into another drop, making one big one, which ran all the way to the bottom of the glass, making a little puddle on the tablecloth. The background lunch noise seemed to grow louder in our silence. She lit a cigarette, put her sunglasses on, and stared out the window onto sunny Tinker Street. She swallowed and I watched her throat rippling.

I hadn't wanted to tell her. It didn't make me feel good, or better, or that it gave me a chance or anything. It was just that she hadn't been around for a few weeks, she hadn't heard. Everyone knew. She was gonna hear. So when she got back into town I took her for a drink, and I told her: about his brother's wedding, how he'd met Jane again up there, the proposal. When I got to the word "married" the glass stopped halfway to her lips, the foam beginning to tilt, and she looked up at me and said slowly, "He...got *married?*"

I lit a cigarette and watched her. Not a single tear ran down from under the dark pink glasses. "Oh well," she said after a while, and raised a finger at a passing waitress. "Wild Turkey," she said.

It was dark when we got back to the house, and Skye was about as drunk as I'd ever seen her. I was making coffee in the kitchen when she swayed in, her hip catching on the doorframe. She was holding the heavy disc with a blank label. "Why's so heavy?" she said, hiccupping a little in the middle.

"It's a test pressing," I said, not turning from the sink.

"Of what?"

So we listened to it, neither of us saying anything. When Richard was singing "In a Station," the song about Overlook Mountain, I looked over and saw that her head her was down and her shoulders were shaking. I went over and put my arms around her. "Why didn't you ever tell him?" I asked her, my voice thick.

She took a few deep breaths through her nose and looked up at me, her face, her voice, wet with tears, and said, "Because when he comes into a room I can hardly fucking breathe." Then her head fell down and she started crying again.

Later she fell asleep on the couch and I carried her upstairs—astonished at how little she weighed—and laid her gently on Alex's bed. He was down in New York for a few days for some auditions. I folded the blankets around her, placed my forehead against hers, greedily inhaling her scent: apples, chestnuts, whiskey, and cigarettes. With a rock in my throat I turned the light out, walked along the hall, and got into bed. *"Why didn't you ever tell him?"* Yeah, like it was that simple.

* * *

I woke up, her breath warm on the back of my neck, her hand on my stomach. I went to turn around, but she held me and whispered "Shhh..." so I just laid there, feeling her breasts, belly, and thighs warm against me. We laid like that for a while, our breathing falling into the same rhythm. She ran her hand gently back and forth across my stomach, tracing a pattern with the tips of her nails, and nuzzled into my back, planting soft little kisses on my neck and shoulders. Man, I hadn't expected this, not tonight. Soon enough I couldn't take it anymore and I went fucking crazy; swinging around and kissing her, really kissing her, tearing into her madly, shaking and panting. She climbed on top, took hold of me, guiding me into her, and let out a little cry as she pressed down, her breasts just brushing my face: her eyes were closed and she was biting her lip, her white skin blue in the moonlight. She pressed down one, two, three times and that was it: I was juddering and bucking beneath her, saying "I'm sorry" even as it was happening. She rode it out then bent down, running her face across my face, kissing me some more on the eyes, mouth, nose, cheeks, and said, "No, I'm sorry." It was all over in—maybe—a minute and a half.

* * *

The sun coming through the open window woke me up and I knew from how hot it was that it had to be late. I opened my eyes and turned around slowly, carefully, expecting her to be gone. But she wasn't. She was sleeping with her back to me, her side rising and falling. I laid there and watched her for a long time with a goofy grin on my face. I couldn't believe it, man. I pulled my leg out from under the sheets, feeling the sunlight on my bare skin.

I wanted to get up and dance around, put a record on, play my guitar, and fix breakfast, but I didn't want to wake her up. I was scared she'd get up and leave, scared that, through the gray filter of her hangover, she'd say it had all been a stupid, drunken mistake and head off back to New York. I was scared and happy at the same time. So I just laid there—the sun coming around the house, warming my back now—and stared at her, at the brown mole on the nape of her neck, the downy hair on her arms, and the little puddle of sweat that had collected in the small of her back. After a while she rolled over yawning. I shut my eyes quickly and pretended to be asleep as she nuzzled into me and shook me gently. "Greg?" she whispered. I opened my eyes. Her face was just a few inches away. "I'm hungry."

I went down to the kitchen, trying to remember if we had eggs in the fridge, and opening all the windows in the house on the way, until it felt like the place was just sunshine and clean air. I stopped at the record player to put *Blonde on Blonde* on the turntable and it crossed my mind that it was the first time in weeks that *Music from Big Pink*—that was what they were going to call their album, after the old house on Stoll Road where they wrote it—hadn't been the first record we played in the morning.

The fridge held a lot of beer, but no eggs. I ran back upstairs. "I'm just going to go to the store," I said, pulling on my jeans, burrowing my feet into my sandals.

"OK," she smiled at me, the sheets pulled tight up under her chin.

"Do you want anything special?"

"Food. Lots of food."

I laughed and turned to go. I turned back, "You'll still be here when I get back, right?"

I drove down into Woodstock. Everything looked different—it was like I was in a movie. People all seemed friendlier, kinder. I went to cross the street in front of a parked station wagon and glanced inside. Dylan was at the wheel, his eyes half-closed, sleepy looking. Even on this hot June morning he had all the windows shut tight. I rapped on the hood and he jumped up a little, looked startled and pissed off as I gave him a big wave and a shit-eating grin. Bewildered, he raised three fingers limply from the wheel in acknowledgment and I strolled across the street, chuckling at my own balls. Just as I was getting to my car, Bill Avis came out of Overlook Liquors with a case of beer under his arm. I liked Bill, the band's road manager. He was a solid guy. "Hey Bill, you having a party?"

"Yeah, we're gonna barbecue later. Come on by if you like."

"Maybe, thanks."

"Hey," he said, turning back, shifting the case to his other arm. "You know that whole Warhol, New York crowd, don't you?"

"Little bit. How come?"

"Shit, haven't you heard?"

As I came screeching around our drive I could already hear "*Take a load off Fanny...*" pounding out the open windows. I ran into the house. Skye was just out of the bath. It looked like she'd managed to use every towel in the place; one around her, one on the floor, her hair turbaned in another, and a fourth getting used to pat her face, sweat beaded on her perfect forehead. I kissed her quickly, took the needle off, turned on the TV and started flipping channels. "Hey," she said, flicking a towel at me. "I was listening to that!"

"Look," I tossed her the *New York Times* from under my arm. She looked at the front page and said "Oh my God!" at the same moment I found a news bulletin on a New York Station: a reporter, standing in front of Beth Israel hospital, saying, *"...Well, Jane, he is said to be still in a critical condition with doctors now performing emergency surgery..."*

Valerie Solanas. I was sure I knew her name, from my time with Manny. Yesterday, around the time Skye and I were getting drunk, this chick walked into the Factory and fucking blew him away. *"...shooting Warhol in the chest and escaping before later surrendering herself to the authorities..."*

A shot of her came up on the screen, looking crazy, like everybody does on those kind of photos. Dark-haired, thin, wired-looking: like any one of a bunch of skanky junkie whores who hung around panhandling at the Factory.

"Fuck, man, I think I met that chick."

"Rilly? Why do you think she did it?"

"Who knows? There were always a lot of crazy motherfuckers around that place."

The phone rang and it was Alex. He'd been trying to call all last night but we'd unplugged the phone. He said he'd run into Paul Morrissey on Union Square a few hours after it all went down; Morrissey said he'd been there, he'd heard the shots. Everybody was going fucking nuts, talking about trying to get hold of Solanas before the cops did and handing out a little rough justice. Man, you had to crack up at that one, the Factory lynch mob: like, Viva, Morrissey, the Velvets, and a bunch of transvestites and speed-freaks tearing around Soho with fuckin' baseball bats and burning nooses. "What was he like?" Skye asked, nodding to a file photo of Warhol on the screen.

"I only met him a couple of times," I shrugged, "and there were lots of other people there. He didn't really say anything much."

"Like Dylan," Skye said, sitting down on my lap, putting her arms around me.

Yeah. Dylan, Robertson, Grossman, Neuwirth, Warhol, Reed. All these guys who'd really gotten hold of the idea that conversation was about the uncoolest thing ever. "Yeah, I guess," I said, smiling, pulling the towel off her.

We wound up dragging my mattress downstairs and making a bed up right there on the living room floor—so we could keep checking TV updates on the Warhol thing, so we didn't have to go too far to change the music, get a drink from the icebox, or some more of the meatloaf I'd made from the stove—like kids making a fort.

I woke up in the middle of the night, both of us curled up on the mattress, bathed in the fizz of the TV screen. I laid there for a while, very conscious of my good fortune and how fragile it probably was, reminding myself that she was still in love with this other guy and that I didn't know quite why all this was happening like it was. I crawled along the mattress to turn the TV off. On the screen another news reporter was talking, standing in front of the hospital. Shit I thought; old Andy's a fuckin' draw, man. He's been on all night. Then I noticed the hospital was different: there were palm trees in front of it. Then there was a shot of a big hotel, The Ambassador. Blue light circles flashing on cop cars and police tape all around the place. I crawled over to turn the sound up and Skye moaned and turned away. A photo of a dark-skinned, kind of Arabic looking guy came up and the announcer was saying, "...*shooting the senator three times. The LAPD have now officially named Sirhan Sirhan, a Palestinian Arab, as the sole assassin...*" It cut back to the newsreader in the studio, shaking his head at his monitor, looking numb. There was a big photo of Bobby Kennedy in the corner of the screen. He was gazing off into the distance, looking thoughtful. "Skye," I whispered, nudging her awake, "you ain't gonna believe this..."

Twelve

"Turn the stern, and point to shore..."

My arms were hanging limp over the sides, my hands wrist-deep in the warm, clean water. By paddling a little now and again against the gentle current in the pool I could keep myself floating right underneath the big strip of sunlight that came shining down through the tall, green pines, the black rubber of the big inner tube—Tommy had gotten a bunch of them from somewhere—warm against the back of my neck, knees, arms. I could hear the others laughing and goofing around along the bank—Alex strumming a guitar, playing a stupid, jokey version of "Mrs. Robinson"—the smell of burning joints and sun cream coming toward me on the warm breeze that drifted low across the water. The guys had got a fire going and Skye and Jeannie were grilling chicken and sausage, so there were those smells too.

Man, there were lots of great swimming holes up around Woodstock: places in the woods where big streams came barreling and frothing down into deep pools that were carved out of the rocky ground. There were natural waterfalls that you could shower under; tall trees grew thick all along the banks and sometimes you'd even hear deer running through the woods. I shifted a little, trying to stay in the sunlight, and spilled a little beer from the can resting on my stomach. A drop of it ran cold around my side and into the hollow of my back. I heard a cry and looked up; Johnny and Tommy were throwing Susie naked and screaming into the creek. It was real hot now. I rolled over and tumbled into the water, diving down deep to the bottom of the pool, a silvery chill flashing through me as the water got colder toward the bottom, making my temples pulse. I held onto a big, slippery boulder on the bottom and opened my eyes in time to see the tail of a fat catfish flicking, driving it off into the darkness a few yards away. It felt great. I'd had a fucked up morning.

This kid Donnie I knew, a rich New York kid, had called, sounding fucked up, like he'd been up for a few days, and asked me if I could drop by with some brown. He'd laughed when he'd heard "Chest Fever" playing in the background, he'd got hold of a copy from somewhere—I don't know how, it wasn't out yet—and had it on too.

It had become routine that summer: the first person up the morning, usually me, sometimes Alex, now again it would be Skye or Susie, would put the record on full volume, usually side two first off. That was how I woke up every day for weeks, laying in bed—on my own, sometimes with Skye—with "We Can Talk" thumping up against the floorboards, the sun coming in through my thin, green curtains, turning the room underwater colors, glinting off the strings and tuning pegs of my Martin. Gradually, as the summer wore on, you'd go around people's houses and realize that everyone who'd gotten an advance copy had the same routine.

The weather got finer and more people kept arriving in Woodstock and heroin was getting to be something I kept around regularly. I wasn't using the little honey-pot anymore. Sometimes I had as much as a quarter ounce in that hollow under my wardrobe, stuffed down there with the tightly banded cash, the pills, grass, coke, and Alex's .22 Woodsman. I wasn't using too much myself, just smoking and snorting some here and there. I hadn't shot up again since that first time with my dad. All kinds of people we knew were using junk—I was probably seeing a little more of Levon on nonsocial terms than was strictly healthy, but I don't think he was shooting up yet either.

Supply wasn't a problem: the Tenth Avenue guys were starting to get more and more of this shit in. Business was booming for them too. You were starting to see a lot of crazy, twitchy-looking guys in frayed, stained olive-green combat jackets—names like Khe Sanh and Ia-Drang embroidered and stencilled on the sleeves and on the back—coming up and down that dark, piss-soaked stairwell. You'd get out of their fucking way, man.

So, Donnie called and a couple of hours later I came along the drive through the woods—which took a while, the place was set back in a couple of hundred acres—and pulled up in front of the place, a huge blue-stone mansion that belonged to some friends of Donnie's parents. (Donnie's dad was something big on Madison Avenue.) There was a hippie couple lying on the front lawn, talking and stroking each other. The guy didn't have any pants on. The front door was hanging open and music was coming from inside the house.

The hallway led into this big, vaulted living room, lots of

wood and stone, windows all along one wall looking out onto the gardens. The curtains were closed and it was dark, a lot of people were running around, the party still going full tilt from the night before. A movie projector was showing some film on a sheet draped over one wall. The music was loud, the Airplane doing "White Rabbit." I took my sunglasses off and was squinting around, looking for Donnie, when a chick came up to me; blonde, cute, naked. Her breasts—surprisingly heavy for her size, with big dark nipples—and stomach were glistening, slick and sticky with something. It didn't look like cum.

"Do you want some?" she asked me, and I saw now that she was holding one of those clear plastic honey bears.

"No, I'm good. Have you seen Donnie?"

"You don't want some?" she said, sad and surprised as she smeared another handful across her stomach, her eyeballs fizzing around, like they were trying to bust loose from the sockets.

"No baby. Have you seen Donnie? *Don-ee?*" I raised my voice above Grace Slick bawling, *"Feed your head,"* speaking to her like you would to a child or a retard. She looked me up and down slowly for a minute.

"Are you a cop?" she asked finally.

"Yeah," I sighed. "I'm a cop. Go get your fuckin' clothes on, you're under arrest, bitch." I walked off, leaving her standing there honey dripping from her tits onto the floor.

There were about a dozen people in the living room, some dancing, some lying spaced out on the floor and sofas. A kid was just puking right in the middle of the room. I lifted a big cowboy hat up and had a look at the guy passed out underneath but I didn't recognize him. I was thinking about just leaving when Donnie came along the hall with his arm around this girl Marcy we knew. "Greg!"

"What the fuck Donnie?"

"Yeah," he looked around, smiling at the carnage. "Tony, you know Tony right? He came up from California a couple of days ago with a suitcase full of the craziest fucking acid you ever took. I mean, instant lobotomy shit. So..." he gestured around. "Anyway, come on through," he started off down the hall and turned to Marcy, "Hey baby, can you get me and Greg a couple of drinks, vodka right?"

"Yeah."

"Same for me baby. We'll be in the den. Thanks for coming over man." He put an arm around me. "I don't really know these guys, they turned up with some chicks. I think one of them is a friend of Dylan's. They couldn't get hold of their regular guy..."

We went into the den. Two big brocade sofas faced each other across a coffee table. The table—a massive slab of granite—was covered with bottles, glasses, porno magazines, ashtrays, syringes, belts. A few guys—mostly older than me, late twenties, early thirties—and a couple of chicks were sitting facing each other, talking bullshit. "Ahh shit," I thought when I saw Bobby Neuwirth. He could be a mean, nasty son of a bitch in these situations. I recognized one of the other guys too, John somebody; some actor or poet who knew Mason Hoffenberg, the writer, Dylan's buddy. I'd seen him talking to Levon at a party one night.

It was a scene I'd walked into hundreds of times in the last four or five years, definitely one of the more fucked up aspects of doing what I did: walking into places at dawn, or the next afternoon, when you're straight and they're still doing whatever the fuck they've been for doing for two or three days: all shaking and sweating, one wheel left on the fuckin' wagon.

As we came over Neuwirth went "Shhh..." and put a finger to his lips, making out like they'd been talking about us. "This is Greg," said Donnie, as I sat down on the end of the sofa.

"Hi there," said John, extending his hand. He had on a nice white shirt, but there were a couple of rusty looking blood stains in the crook of the elbow. "We were just discussing, which is the more powerful medium, music or film? What do you think?" Neuwirth and the others smiled expectantly at me. Oh man, one of these deals where you know there's no right answer. I decided to play it country simple.

"Well, I wouldn't know about that. I'm just a drug dealer. Would you like to buy some drugs?"

There was a pause and then they started laughing, except Neuwirth, who'd been scenting blood and who looked disappointed. "Well, let's see what you got kid," said one guy. In my inside left was the cut Tenth Avenue heroin. In the inside right was the uncut shit I got from Dave. The real deal. Fucking powdered Khe Sanh. I reached into the inside right and handed a wrap to him, saying, "You might wanna be careful with that." They all laughed as he started tapping some out and John started prepping a needle.

Five fuckin' minutes later and three of us—me, John, and Donnie—are crashing around the bathroom, trying to get the guy underneath the shower. Neuwirth had disappeared the moment he passed out, falling forward face down into the granite coffee table twenty seconds after the spike went in. John was slapping his face real hard, almost punching him, and yelling at Donnie. "Get some fucking ice, man!" Donnie turned and screamed "MARCY! GET SOME FUCKING ICE CUBES!"

We laid him down on the bathroom floor, his head and shoulders inside the shower stall, and turned freezing water on him. Nothing. I grabbed a hold of his face and pulled an eyelid open. The pupil was so small it might as well not be there. His lips were turning blue. "Larry! Larry!" Brent was shouting, still slapping him, *"Come on, man!"* One of the guy's buddies turned to me and said, "What the fuck, man?"

"I fuckin' tried to tell him!"

"Yeah? You should have—"

"Hey! Shut the fuck up!" said John. He pulled Larry's pants down and a big slick of shit poured out across the floor. It didn't look like he'd been eating too good. Marcy came running into the room with a silver ice bucket, cubes clattering and skidding across the tiled floor. There was a crowd, a hippie freak show in the doorway now; tripping kids, the guy in the cowboy hat, the naked, honey-covered chick, the Doors playing in the background. Marcy gave John the ice bucket and threw up. John grabbed a towel and wiped a load of the shit away from Larry's ass. He and I looked at each other. I shook my head. No way, man, I didn't even know the fuckin' guy. "Ah, fuck it," he said.

He turned Larry onto his side, spread his cheeks with one hand, grabbed a handful of ice with the other, and jammed a couple of big chunks up his dirty asshole, pushing them home with his thumb. He had a third piece halfway in when Larry's asshole protested, contracting—like the beak of a squid I'd seen once in a nature film—and shooting the ice cube back out. It skittered across the bathroom floor, leaving little brown, watery marks on the white tiles. John rammed another chunk up there and Larry's left leg trembled, then kicked, and he jerked up a little opening his eyes and coughing. John held onto his hair and shook his head around, keeping him under the cold shower, keeping him awake, keeping him alive, as the heroin tried to take him all the way down.

"Wow," said Donnie, laughing. "Did you see that, man? It came outta his ass like a fucking bullet! Do it again, man!"

John wiped his brow, using the back of the hand that hadn't been up his buddy's ass, and said, "I had to do that for William Burroughs once..."

I was turning the engine on when John came around the house, walking slowly. It took him a while to reach me. "You were right," he said, leaning against the warm black Corvette, "that stuff is fucking good..." I gave him my number, writing it out on the back of a matchbook from Deanie's, and drove off. The couple on the grass in front of the house were fucking now, the girl on top, laughing her ass off as she rode him. She gave me a little wave as I drove past and I honked the horn, laughing too. It always looked real peaceful as you drove through the mountains along those dusty gravel roads cut through all the greenery, but, man, was there some crazy shit going on in those big houses back in the woods.

I came barreling up out of the water and threw myself back across the warm tire. "Hey Greg," Skye called from the bank, "you wanna sausage?" She was waving a burnt looking link on a stick; I shook my head and she laughed. I floated there, watching her and Jeannie getting the food ready, Tommy and Johnny play fighting on the bank, trying to chuck each other in, Warren, Alex, and Susie singing "Like a Rolling Stone." It was a nice scene.

Skye and I got together, Warhol lived, and Kennedy died. (We found out later that Dylan's old man back in Minnesota had died the same day as Kennedy, the same day I saw him snoozing at the wheel of his station wagon on Tinker Street.) Was she my girlfriend? She was around most weekends. She'd come home with me at the end of the night and we'd get in bed together. She'd call me from New York or Vermont every few days when she was away. I learned things about her.

She'd grown up with servants and cooks.

She loved NY street corner hotdogs. (Extra sauerkraut.)

She couldn't sing.

She liked sex when she woke up.

She had two older brothers on Wall Street and a younger sister at Camden.

She had no idea what she was going to do when she graduated. (Probably Europe.)

She could do a good British accent.

She'd lost her driver's licence the first year she had it. DUI.

Sometimes when we were out in company, in Deanie's or someplace, and we'd wind up near Richard and Jane she'd be normal. She said it had just been a stupid crush, that she was probably more in love with the guy's voice than anything else.

Was she my girlfriend? I wasn't about to ask that. It was just fine the way it was. I'd take it. No questions, man, no questions.

Thirteen

"The Flying Dutchman's on the reef..."

It was a Saturday in August, so hot the air singed your nostrils and the vinyl bucket seats of the Corvette scalded the backs of legs as you sat down. I had a whole bunch of shit to do: I had to drop by Spencer Road with some stuff for Richard. I had to drive out toward Kingston to meet this guy Bobby who owed me money. I needed to swing by the garage to get a new oil filter. Skye was back from Vermont for the weekend; we were having a barbecue for Alex's birthday later on. I had to get to the supermarket to pick up chicken, sausages, and bread. I pulled off Spencer Road and parked under some trees, to keep the sun off the car.

The record was breaking out and now the guys weren't just famous around Woodstock anymore. They were getting properly famous: *Time* magazine, *Life* magazine, the *New York fuckin' Times*, were all falling all over the place saying how great they were. They weren't called The Crackers anymore either. They'd decided just to call themselves "The Band." I didn't like that name too much either. Neither did Levon. He was still rooting for The Crackers. But The Band, I don't know, man. You could have said it was a little lazy, or maybe desperate, or just too plain "big-dicked." ("Yeah you might be in *a* band, but we're *The* Band," I said. "Hell," Richard growled, "it's only a fucking name.") But, whatever, it stuck. You soon got used to it.

The guys themselves didn't really change—except maybe Robbie managed to cram himself a little bit further up his own ass—but people around them started to change. By the end of the summer there were more and more dealers in town, more chicks, more faces wanting a place at the fireside.

I walked around the house, music—Junior Parker—drifted from open windows out over the fields. Richard was stretched out in the blazing grass around back, reading a newspaper. They had a great view here, down across baking treetops, across green fields dotted with buttery splashes of dandelions and out over the Ashokan, twenty square miles of still, flat water glittering like a spilt bag of jewels under the summer sun. He looked up as I came rustling through the grass and said, "Hot enough for ya?"

"Shit, I nearly got third degree burns from the goddamn car seat."

"Listen to this, man." He folded the paper over—it was this new magazine, *Rolling Stone*—and read from it in a pompous sarcastic voice. "This album was recorded in approximately two weeks. There are people who will work their lives away in vain and not touch it."

"What album?"

"Ours, man!"

"Shit," I said, taking it from him.

"It ain't *that* fucking good! I mean this," he nodded into the air, at Parker's tight, punchy grooves, "now this is good."

"Yours is pretty good too, man." I hadn't been able to find the right moment, or the right words, to tell him just how good it was. How good *he* was. Robbie's stuff was great—it was his "take a load off Fanny" song everyone was singing, that they were playing on the radio—but it was Richard's sad songs, sung in his breaking, quivering voice, that really did it for me. But it was difficult to say the words because Richard squirmed under compliments; he twisted and pulled away from them, like a child who doesn't want to be kissed by his aunt at Christmas.

"The next one's going to be better anyway," he said, getting up. "You wanna beer?"

They were talking about going to California to make their next album. We were talking about California too.

After you've lived in the Catskills a while you start to fear the winter around the beginning of September. This would be Alex's fourth, my third. Alex was figuring on getting an agent in LA. He'd heard there was plenty of work; commercials, bit parts: a couple hundred bucks a day for walking in a straight line past the camera. Skye would be graduating next spring, she was thinking about doing her Masters at UCLA. She hadn't asked me to come out and live with her, in so many words. But she had asked me a couple of times if I was gonna spend the rest of my life "selling fucking drugs." Maybe I could transfer out there from NYU. Retake some courses, finish my degree. But, no, I couldn't see myself finishing the 1960s as a twenty-three-year-old student. I knew a few people out there through Donnie though; I *could* see myself selling drugs to students. Just grass, maybe. Cut back on the heavy stuff. Get an apartment near the ocean. Pick my little honey up after class with the top down all year round. We'd eat salads and pasta and walk on the beach. No more snow tires and stuffing ice up people's assholes.

Richard came back with Jane and a couple of cold beers and we drank them as we watched the heat haze rippling over the reservoir and talked about people we knew and things that were happening. I never talked much about Skye around him. He never knew how she'd felt but I still got uncomfortable when the two of them met in my head. "I gotta run," I said. "Stuff to do. You guys gonna come along later?"

"Sure, thanks Greg," he said, waving goodbye with the plastic baggie of grass I'd brought him. I turned back as I reached the house and looked at him laid out in the sun with his great view, his model wife, his cold beer, and his great *Rolling Stone* review. His talent. *You lucky sumbitch,* I thought to myself, laughing, as I got back in the car.

I had the wind and a big stupid grin on my face as I pulled up in front of our house, fat whitewalls munching on the baking gravel. I skipped up the steps—wondering if I had time to go buy the food for the barbecue before Skye arrived, or would it be fun to go together? Wondering what she'd be wearing—and pushed the screen door open, looking forward to a Coke from the icebox and a few minutes in the cool of house. Alex was sitting on the couch. There was a man standing in front of the fireplace; in his forties, balding, wearing a suit and tie. He looked like a salesman. I pushed my sunglasses up into my hair. Alex went to get up, but the guy put out a hand and stopped him. "Hey," I started to say. Something silver on Alex's wrists caught in the sunlight, glinting.

Handcuffs.

Alex started to cry.

There were footsteps coming down the stairs now and the salesman guy was reaching into his jacket. He pulled out something made of gold and black leather and started talking as two more guys came into the room. They were in uniform and one of them was carrying a shoebox; the one from under my wardrobe. For some reason I wondered where they had parked.

The guy in the suit stood there, holding out his badge and talking—saying the words we all knew from the movies and TV—but I couldn't hear him or see him anymore, because there was a roaring in my head, my legs were buckling, and my peripheral vision was blurring, glittering, and zinging as my pupils widened, like they do just before you have an accident or get into a fight.

They put my hands behind my back. I felt the warm metal sliding around my wrists, clicking into place, pinching the skin, and all I could think was, who's gonna meet Skye?

Fourteen

"It's my belief—we used up all of our time..."

Fishkill Correctional Facility,
Duchess County, NY, December 3, 1973

Today was a bad day. You get good and bad days inside just like anyplace else.

Fucker, my cellmate, told me bad days happened when you either thought too far ahead or something came up that reminded you strongly of life outside, the life you once had. You had to block that shit out, he said. (*"Don't go being no pussy, now. Don't be crying in here."*) He was right. When you just dealt in the here-and-now of your situation—whatever chore you were meant to be doing, the card game you were playing, the book you were reading, the drugs you were taking or scoring—then it wasn't too bad. You could about get along.

This afternoon I was in the little library they have here (a novelty after Rikers. Rikers was no-frills. Rikers was fuckin' Coach. New York City, it turned out, was a toilet. The upstate prisons like Fishkill were the cesspool it ran into. Rikers was the fuckin' u-bend: it all caught there at some point. It was the worst kind of cluster fuck: 15,000 rapists, murderers, car thieves, dope dealers, mobsters, burglars, muggers, kiddie fuckers all crammed onto a half a square mile rock in the East River. All of New York State's problems on an island off the coast of Queens. Nobody knows what's happening, everyone's tense, pre-trial brittle. All the usual prison shit—the shit you hear about—happened on Rikers and some of it happened to me), looking for something to read. There wasn't much of a choice: old Westerns, thrillers, and crime stories. Tattered copies of *Life* and *Newsweek*, like a dentist's waiting room from 1965. I was flipping through a stack of magazines when I saw the words "The Band" printed bold across a strange cartoon. I didn't recognize anyone at first: Garth's and Levon's beards were enormous. Richard looked like a pirate, like Blackbeard or something, with one half of his face in darkness and a wide-brimmed hat on.

A line running diagonally across the top right of the picture said "The New Sound of Country Rock." It was *Time* magazine. The front fuckin' cover. I looked at the dateline in the top right hand corner of the page: January 12, 1970.

Nearly four years ago.

It all came running on into my head—the life I once had—and I went back to the cell to try and sleep or something. But sleep wouldn't come, and I couldn't shake it off. I thought about trying to talk to Fucker about it, about how these guys I used to know were on the cover of *Time* magazine. Then I looked across at him—200 pounds of angry nigger reading a busted-up, cum-spackled copy of *Sluts*, a gook chick on the cover with a foot-long prick splitting her face in half—and I thought, "No."

I'd only cried once before inside, on Rikers: New Years Eve '69. It was just starting to get dark and we were out in the exercise yard. I was standing on my own, staring out through the rusted chain-link fence into the freezing black chop of the East River at the whitecaps collapsing into each other when a Puerto Rican kid I knew—a nineteen-year-old doing a year for GTA—came up and nudged me. "Hey, look over there, man."

I followed his gaze across the water, past south Bronx toward Manhattan. It was dusk and lights were coming on in apartment buildings. "People, they gonna be celebrating the nineteen-seventays tonight!" the kid said. You could picture them; polishing glasses, putting out dip, making sure they had enough ice, putting a record on. Yeah, south Bronx, down into Harlem, past Columbia, then the northern tip of Central Park. Central Park: the Dakota Building. Snorting coke and drinking rum at a millionaire's party. Columbia University: Skye. She'd written me a lot the first year. She'd wanted to visit. I kept saying no and, finally, the letters stopped coming.

I'd grabbed onto the fence with both hands and let my head drop onto my chest. My shoulders started shaking. "Man, are you..." said Timmy, "...that's fucked up. You lucky I'm the only motherfucker here." He walked away quickly.

This time I waited until Fucker was asleep on the bunk below me. I turned into the wall, stuffed my face into the pillow, and cried hard and quiet for a long time.

* * *

It was Johnny Becker.

He'd been pulled over for speeding on the Glasco

Turnpike by a state trooper. He'd been making some deliveries; a pound of grass, a bunch of speed, and a couple of grams of junk under his seat. Apparently he'd fumbled his drivers license and dropped it on the floor of the car. The trooper—a helpful Ulster County guy—had bent down to help him look for it and saw shiny cellophane tucked away. They took him to the station in Kingston and called the DEA. It didn't take them long to figure out Johnny had jumped bail in California on a dope offense. He was looking at twenty years, minimum. It didn't take him long to give me up.

They found the shoebox: another quarter ounce of heroin, coke, acid, diet pills, three different kinds of weed, a handgun, and around five thousand dollars in cash.

I wasn't noble for too long. I gave up my Tenth Avenue guys as soon as they dangled a deal in front of me. But that took a couple of days; by then word about me and Johnny being arrested had trickled down to people we knew in the city. When the cops bust down the door all they found was an empty apartment building. All I had was that address, so now all they had was me.

The judge listened for a long time as the public defender read from a social report that said I was an educated boy who'd made a foolish mistake and that I hoped one day to return to a promising college career.

Yeah, he listened. He nodded. He poured himself a glass of water and drank some of it off. He rapped his notes on the bench, cleared his throat, and gave me twelve years.

Fifteen

"The hill's too steep to climb..."

Los Angeles, 1977

It was my first time in California and, yeah, I was over-dressed. I was wearing a thick flannel shirt, T-shirt, and heavy jeans. I unbuttoned the shirt all the way down and flapped it, fanning myself, as traffic blew by on Santa Monica Boulevard, dust and exhaust fumes blasting across the sidewalk a few yards away.

I sipped my beer and fidgeted, waiting for Alex to get back. It was lunchtime and the tables outside were crowded with tanned people drinking white wine and mineral water, eating salads and grilled chicken. All around me muted laughter, chiming cutlery, and the smell of food. I was hungry, a side effect of prison. When you got out you wanted to eat *all the time*. The day I got out of Fishkill—three weeks ago now—I rode the Greyhound down to New York and went straight into a diner near the Port Authority Bus Terminal. I ate three enormous cheeseburgers—roiling in grease, fried onions falling out of 'em—a plate of chili fries, a serving of onion rings, and two thick slices of cherry cheesecake. I drank about a quart of scalding coffee and the same of chilled OJ. I sat back, popped open my belt, and lit a cigarette. Seconds later I was staggering around in the alleyway behind the joint, throwing up for a long, long time.

It was still strange to be out, to be walking around on my own and doing whatever I liked. It felt like when you're sixteen and you get your license and drive a car on your own for the first time; exhilarating and scary, like you shouldn't really be doing this alone, that there should be someone else—an adult—with you.

A long, fat limousine the color of a fridge cruised by, a girl's hand—long painted fingernails, gold bangles—dangling out the window holding a cigarette, and Alex came back, weaving between tables, ignoring a couple of chicks who were trying to get his attention. He sat down and knocked a Lucky Strike out of my pack. "Sorry about that, man," he said, lighting it.

"That's OK. You're busy."

We'd done the catching up thing that morning, when I turned up—unannounced at seven a.m., straight off the fuckin' bus—on the doorstep of his apartment in Brentwood. He was letting me crash on his couch for a few days, save me a couple of bucks.

"Did you get that number?" I asked.

He shook his head, "She didn't have it; I got the address though." He handed me scrap of paper that said "300065 MORNING VIEW DRIVE, ZUMA BEACH."

"Thanks, man."

"No problem. It's out past Santa Monica. Take the Pacific Coast Highway north through Malibu."

"Right." I finished my beer and fumbled in my pocket.

"Hey, fuck off, man. I got it," Alex said.

"You sure?"

"Yeah. I'll stick it on my tab."

"Thanks Alex. Well, I'll see you tonight I guess." I got up, taking my denim jacket from the back of the chair.

"Listen, I'm sorry about your guitar, man."

"Don't worry about it. I haven't played in years anyway." I put my jacket on, pointlessly.

"Look, Greg," he said, getting up too, moving nearer me, "don't go expecting too much out there. They're big stars now, you know, man?"

"Yeah, I know. I just want to say hi."

"OK, man. I'll see you later."

Alex turned and picked up a tray. He started loading glasses and plates onto it. I guess I should have been mad at him for selling my guitar to pay off some dealer, but I wasn't. It was just wood and steel. I could buy another.

I wasn't too worried about money: my dad had died a couple of years back. He was sixty-five and had been a junkie for twenty-one years. I never saw him again after my mom's funeral. I got a letter from his lawyer saying he'd left me the house, some savings, a few stocks and bonds. It was all worth about $20,000 Canadian. So I'd be OK for a while, until I figured out what I was going to do.

A woman signalled Alex and he put the tray down and went over to her, taking a pad and pen from his back pocket to write her order down. She knew what she wanted; rhyming off the dishes, counting them on her fingers, probably telling him to hold stuff and to put different shit on the side, like these old cunts always did. It was fuckin' strange to see Alex serving people, man. Parts were hard to get, he said.

* * *

Alex had lent me his car, a rusted old Pinto. You had to drive careful he said; the clutch was nearly gone. But I was driving careful anyway: braking gently at the first sign of a yellow light, waiting forever before I made turns across traffic, pulling away slowly, indicating properly, and shit like that. I was driving like the kind of old guy I used to hate getting stuck behind.

After wrong turning and dead-ending around Topanga Park for a while I came down Pacific Palisades and made a right onto the highway, the ocean big and green on my left, mountains on my right. I turned the radio on and got some girl singing *"Don't stop, thinking about tomorrow"* over and over, a song you were hearing everywhere. I didn't know much about all the new music. I let that part of me die when I was in prison. If you tried to remain the person you were you went nuts. You saw it happening all the time. You have to give it up, become something else, this other version of you. The week before, back in New York, I'd been staggering along 42nd Street, blinking into a cold wind, when I passed a bunch of kids on the corner of Seventh. They looked worse than I did coming straight out of the joint: ripped jeans, torn up sneakers, fucked up hair. One of them had a T-shirt on that said "piss." Punk Rock, they called it. It was happening downtown and over in England. It didn't seem to make much sense, man: a bunch of fuckin' fruits screaming and pissing their pants.

I took the left marked "Zuma Beach," parked the car, and wandered down, smelling the salt of the ocean. You could hear the waves. There was a big equipment truck parked along the lane, two guys were unloading poles and lamps, lighting equipment of some sort. A little sign said "300065 MORNING VIEW." I nodded to them and walked on toward the big ranch house acting like I knew what I was doing. No one stopped me. The front door was open and I walked straight in. It was kind of dark in the hallway, with plum-colored, thick velvet wallpaper. It looked like a fuckin' whorehouse. Two guys came marching down the narrow corridor toward me, one carrying a camera and the other a big microphone that looked like a huge, fur-covered pill. "Excuse me!" the first guy said, sweeping past me. He turned back to the other guy and said, "Same shit, every fucking day, man..." They went on outside. I walked on down the hall. There was music in the distance.

I passed a doorway and looked in. Garth Hudson was watching TV, the windows in the room open onto the beach and the ocean. He hadn't aged a day in ten years. I mean, he'd always looked old, so he didn't look any different now he was old. I guessed Garth would have to be in his forties now. I knocked on the doorframe and he turned around. "Uh, hi Garth," I began.

"Can I help you?" he asked, neither annoyed or pleased.

"Uh, it's Greg?" Nothing. "Greg Keltner? From Woodstock?" His face cleared a little.

"Hi. How are you?"

"Ah, good. I was in town and thought I'd swing by and say hi. I...I was away for a while, you know? How's things? How's it all going?"

"Slowly," he smiled.

"Do you know if Richard's around?"

"He's probably still in bed. If you go back out the door and follow the path down around the house, you'll see a little bungalow. Give the door a knock."

"Right. Thanks Garth. Good to see you."

"Sure." He gave me a little wave and turned back to the television.

I'd been knocking for a while. I was nervous, felt like some guy looking up an old girlfriend, wondering if her husband's going to answer the door. Finally, there was some muffled shouting from inside, the sound of someone falling around, a bottle breaking. The door yanked open and there was Richard. To be honest I only recognized him because I'd seen some recent pictures in *Rolling Stone*. The guy standing in front of me in a stained T-shirt and underpants bore no relation to the guy I'd known before. He had a wild bushy beard, bits of gray running through it, crusts of food caught in it. His skin was the color of a ripe banana and he was so thin. But there was no mistaking those eyebrows, dark, furry, raised in irritated anticipation. "Yeah?" he said. "What do you fucking want, man?" His voice was a thick, cracked growl.

"It's Greg, Richard. Greg Keltner." He squinted, his eyes refocusing in the clean California sunshine and stared at me for a few more seconds, wheels turning as he rolodexed through the thousands of people he'd probably met in a decade of hit records, world tours, and parties. "*Shit, man,*" he finally said, stumbling forward and hugging me. He smelled bad.

The Band had retired from live work, quit the road, he said. They'd played their last ever concert last Thanksgiving in

San Francisco. A lot of big stars showed up and played with them: Dylan, Neil Young, Van Morrison, Joni Mitchell. They'd made a movie of it, *The Last Waltz*, they called it. They were still making a movie of it. "Goddamned thing ain't ever gonna be finished," Richard said. "So how come you decided to stop playing?" I asked him. We were in the little living room. The curtains were drawn tight against the clean California sunshine, the room dark and fetid; clothes, pizza boxes, Chinese food cartons, ashtrays, empty liquor bottles all over the floor, couch, table. Richard was prowling around looking for glasses.

"Fucked if I know, man. It's Robbie's thing, this movie, the whole deal..." He found a glass and a bottle and came over, threw some clothes on the floor and sat down opposite me. "Listen Greg, I meant to say, I'm sorry I didn't write you more. When you were inside. I meant to, it's just we..."

"Hey, fuck that. C'mon, let's have a drink."

He poured a shot of something into a dirty glass, his hands ticking and trembling, and passed it to me. "Cheers." He didn't have a glass, just clinked the bottle against mine and took a long drink from the neck. I knocked it back tasting something orange, sweet, and burning at the same time. "Shit..." I said, coughing.

"Grand Marnier. Breakfast of champions!" Richard said. "You wanna line?"

I hadn't taken cocaine in almost nine years. "Yeah," I said. He picked a big mirror up off the floor and pulled out a huge bag of coke; half an ounce easy. "Man, you guys must be doing OK!" I said, laughing.

"Yeah, well," he chuckled, "we're signing with Warner Brothers when the Capitol deal finishes. They put us on this retainer thing, two thousand bucks a week."

"That ain't bad five ways."

"No, man—two thousand a week *each*. For the next two years! For doing jack shit." He snorted and pushed the mirror toward me, the fucking line looked like an elephant's leg. I did half of it and felt the strong rush right away, my throat constricting like I was gonna throw up.

Richard woke up, getting excited. "The thing is, the thing is, I don't think it'll really be forever. We'll take a couple of years off and then come back again. Robbie's just burned out. Him and Lee ain't getting along. We just need some time off."

"Yeah?"

"Yeah. We need to play, man. It's in the blood. He'll come around. Lemme get dressed and I'll show you around the studio." He opened the curtains and started rooting through piles of clothes, sniffing things, trying to find something to wear. The daylight made the room look about a hundred times worse, there were cigarette burns everywhere, overflowing ashtrays, stains on the carpet. Jane had left him, taking the kids, about a year back. He couldn't remember exactly when it had happened.

There was a knock at the door. "Come in," Richard shouted. A girl popped her head around, she didn't come all the way into the room. She was pretty, young, holding a clipboard. "Ah, hi Richard. Martin's asked me to see if you can do this interview this afternoon."

"Yeah, I'll do it later."

"Uh, right. Can I tell him when later?"

"Later."

She took it in: me, the bottles, the mirror, the coke, and said, "OK. Thanks." She left.

He picked up the straw and pulled the mirror back toward him, for a moment as it slid across the low table both of our faces were caught there, reflected among the pearly, flaky powder. As Richard bent down, his own face coming up to meet him, the straw from its nostril, meeting the one from his, a gull cried right outside the window. Somewhere close by a radio was playing, *"Don't stop, thinking about tomorrow..."* the same song I'd heard on the way over, the music carried across the beach to us by the same sea breeze that ruffled the curtains behind my head, bringing the salt and wood tang of the beach into the little cottage. But I couldn't smell it anymore, on account of all the coke.

It hit me that I'd probably never get to see them play.

There was a party later on. I met Ron Wood, Ringo Starr, a bunch of other guys. They were all buddies of Richard and Rick's. Everyone got wrecked.

I was coming back from the john, having just thrown up, when I saw two guys coming along the hallway toward me. One of them was tall, the other tiny, bearded. The small one was frantically explaining something in a hushed voice to the tall guy, who stooped to listen. He was well dressed, a cool-looking, expensive leather jacket on, an open-necked silk shirt, and fresh blue jeans. As they got closer I saw the tall guy was Robertson. The girl with the clipboard and a couple of other people were following them. Robbie looked me quickly up and down as they brushed past, the little guy still jabbering away at him. He didn't recognize me and I didn't say anything. He looked like a movie star now; tanned, thick layered hair, aviator sunglasses. ·

Rick was real friendly though, real pleased to see me. He

was making a solo record and asked me if I wanted to play guitar on a track. "Nah," I said. "I haven't played in years." So we sat drinking and snorting and talking about the old days for a while before I asked him, "Hey, did you ever hear from Skye?"

"Shit, Skye. I saw her one time, a few years back. It was in...shit, was it San Diego? No, San Francisco, in '74 on the tour we did with Bob. She came to see the show and came backstage afterward with her husband, some kind of real estate guy, friend of Bill Graham's."

"How was she?"

"All grown up now, man. It was weird. She was so fuckin' crazy back then..." We both shook our heads and didn't say anything.

The sun was coming up and there was just me and Richard left, like so many times in the old days, back in Woodstock. "Let's go for a walk on the beach," I said. I'd never seen the Pacific before. "Shit," groaned Richard, "do we have to?" But he put his sandals on. We both did a big hit of coke, he picked up another bottle of the sickly orange brandy, and we went out through the studio. The live room had big sliding doors that pretty much opened straight onto the sand.

We stumbled across the beach. I took my shoes and socks off and we walked along the surf line, the wet sand still cold, slimy between my toes, but the water warmish around my ankles. In the mid-distance a guy was running toward us. I nudged Richard, worried. "What the fuck's he running for?"

"He's a jogger, man. You see them around here."

"What the fuck is a jogger?"

"People who run, you know, they run for the, ah, for the exercise I guess."

"Shit." The guy passed came close to us and Richard gave him a cheery wave with the squat brown bottle, saying, "Mornin'! How ya' doing?" The guy ran—jogged—straight past us without saying anything. We were laughing our asses off, man.

"Hey," said Richard, "you wanna see Bob's place? It's just along here." He pointed down the beach, back toward Malibu, toward LA. The land curved, jutting out into the water, forming a little peninsula.

"Dylan lives out here too now?"

"Yeah, he owns that whole bit of land," Richard said, pointing to the peninsula. "He's been building this crazy fucking house for years, man. He finally gets it about finished and guess what?"

"What?"

"Sara leaves him!" Richard laughed.

"Shit. How come?"

"Ah, you know Bob. He just couldn't stop fucking chicks. He was practically fucking 'em in front of her, man."

We walked on down the beach and scrambled up a low cliff face and along a path between bushes and rocks. There was a big, high fence surrounding Dylan's property, with a sign saying PRIVATE PROPERTY. ARMED RESPONSE. Just like the kind of thing he had in Woodstock, way back when. Richard was walking along the fence, looking for a way in he said he knew. "Shit Richard, is this a good idea, man?" We weren't in any shape to be climbing fences.

"Yeah, c'mon up. Everywhere round here has those signs, man, it don't mean shit. Just...put your foot there." He'd gotten up a couple of rocks and onto a lower section of fencing. I climbed up beside him. You could see into the grounds. Richard whistled, "Will ya look at that fucking place?"

I grabbed onto the fence and pulled myself up. Holy shit. Out of wood and metal Dylan had built this huge, crazy look- ing mansion, like some kinda space age temple. On top of the house, burning and reflecting in the sun, was an enormous, onion-shaped copper dome, like something you'd see in pho- tos of old buildings in Russia or someplace. It looked like something out of a fairytale. Or a nightmare.

"Man, that's something," I said.

"Ain't it?"

"What's old Bob up to in there?"

"He's editing this movie he's made. With Howard!" We both laughed. Ten years on, man, and Dylan was holed up in another mansion, on the other side of the country, trying to make another fuckin' movie with Howard Alk.

"Should we go in?"

"Nah. Bob drops in on you. You don't drop in on Bob," Richard said, climbing back down.

We got back down onto the beach and sat down, Richard laid back in the sand while I looked out to sea. There were a few yachts out there, their sails white slashes in the endless blue and green. The sun was climbing now, getting hot. Richard had buried the Grand Marnier bottle in the sand to keep it from getting too warm. I twisted it out and took a long pull. There was something I wanted to ask him. Something I'd been thinking about for a few weeks, ever since I got out of jail and went into a record store in New York and bought all the records they'd made when I was gone. I hadn't managed to listen to all of them yet, some of 'em sounded great. Some were just OK. None of them sounded as good to me as that first one they wrote down in the cinder block basement of that old house off Pine Lane, back in '67.

"Richard?" I said, turning to face him. He was lying on his back, sunglasses on, looking straight up into a cloudless sky. "How come you never wrote any more songs?"

He sat up slowly and looked out to sea, running a hand through his crackly, straggly black beard. "Well, Robbie was writing so much good stuff," he shrugged, poking a finger into the sand, drawing lines, circles, looking for a second like a little kid who's been asked why they did something bad. "It's just..." he trailed off, looking out at the sailboats, thinking, while the gulls cried and the ocean sucked at our feet. "It's hard," he said in a thick, cracked voice as he turned to look at me, surf and sky reflected in his sunglasses. "It's so fucking hard. You know?"

I nodded and pressed the sandy bottle into his trembling hand. Yeah, I knew.

It was hard.

Sixteen

"The days that remain..."

Toronto, 1986

I came around, the rug scratchy on the back of my neck, the fallen fleck of plaster a couple of inches from my fingertips, the needle bumping and clacking in the run out groove. The final refrain—*"Any day now, any day now..."*—was turning over and over in my head, which meant that I must have turned the record over at some point, but I couldn't remember doing it.

I switched the stereo off, a crackle and boom as it died, the old valves behind the grille fading from orange to white to cold ash. It was dark out now, lights on in the little houses of Scarborough. I picked up the bindle lying near the needle and spoon. It was empty, not even a chalky film of powder left on the glossy paper. I'd have to go downtown. I had a little money upstairs.

Toronto was still winter-cold in March. "Canada," Levon

said Ronnie Hawkins had told him, back in Arkansas in the fifties, before they came up here for the first time, "is colder than an accountant's heart." The guys all used to quote old Ronnie sometimes. One time Rick had gotten and a haircut and I said to him, "Nice haircut." "Thanks son," Rick said, in a bad Southern accent. "I call it the big dick look." One of Ronnie's.

I looked around the bus stop; an Asian couple, a young white girl, an old black guy. The old guy was hunched up on the plastic seat, buckled under the weight of his overcoat, muffler, and hat. Now and again he'd peek out form the black folds of his winter clothes, glancing east along Kingston to see if the bus was coming yet. It wasn't, so I sat there, my head still gray and muzzled from sleep and heroin, and thought about everything and nothing.

Richard Manuel was dead. He'd hung himself in a Florida motel room. Tied a belt around his neck and split his windpipe, the windpipe he'd used to shape those notes and sing like Ray Charles.

Albert Grossman was dead. His heart burst open a few months back, in the first-class compartment of a flight to London: too much French food, too many lawsuits.

Alex was dead. Freebase OD. Found in a dumpster behind a drugstore on Sunset back in 1980, a few months after I left LA. I'd stayed there for the two and a half years it took us to spend every penny my father left me and all that was left was Toronto, this house, and the welfare checks.

Howard Alk was dead. A few years back. A couple of grains too many tapped into the blackened teaspoon, pull back the plunger—boom. One for pain, two for eternity. He was living alone and it was over the holidays so no one found him for a few days. No one knew if it was an accident, an overdose, or if he'd just had enough. But, you have to figure, guys who've been shooting up for twenty years don't OD like that.

Johnny Becker was dead. Stabbed in Attica in the riots there in '71. I didn't hear about it until a few years later. It didn't make me happy. I wasn't mad at Johnny anymore. Sometimes, in prison, I'd think of the things he used to say when we were all watching TV and it would make me laugh. ("*What the fuck yo laughing at, motherfucker?*" Fucker would growl from the bottom bunk.)

Levon, Garth, and Rick all moved back to Woodstock from LA. I guessed they were doing OK. I couldn't go back there. It was too sad, remembering.

Little Tommy was dead, not long after I went inside. He didn't get to "Vancooover." His number had come up and he'd stumbled on a landmine in the jungle in some other place he couldn't pronounce. Alex had gone home for the funeral. He said he'd wondered what was in the coffin.

Robbie Robertson was alive. He worked in the movie business now. The last time I saw him was at an Elvis Costello show at the Troubador in '78. He was giving some chick his autograph. He looked rich, bored, coked up. I thought about saying hello but, with some people, you kind of know them for a while, then you don't know them anymore. Robertson was as distant as some guy I'd sat next to on an airplane once. *Whythanchewlitteldarlin.* I guess Skye had been right about him.

She was doing fine, I heard. They lived in San Francisco: a big house in Pacific Heights and a bunch of kids. I found out when Alex and I ran into Warren on Sunset Boulevard one night. He had a suit on, worked at one of the studios now, an executive. He was friendly enough, but we were loaded, ripped on base, and he said he didn't have time to come and have a drink with us. He'd call us.

A car pulled up at the lights just past the bus stop. I knew what it was before I looked up; that low, grumbling sound, the engine too much for the frame. There were a couple of kids in the Corvette, cruising along Kingston into town, the black road and the night stretching out before them. The 'vette was a mid-70s model, tomato-red. Not as cool as mine had been. Loud rock and roll came muffled from inside until the kid in the passenger seat rolled down the window to flick a butt out, the orange tip sparking in the night as it hit the sidewalk and rolled into the gutter in front of the bus stop. The music became clearer with the window down and I recognized a song I didn't really like, something that had been a big hit a couple of years back, about "Jack and Diane," two American kids growing up in the heartland. I couldn't remember who sang it. I didn't pay any attention to that stuff anymore. I had enough records.

The lights changed and the car roared off, a line from the song spilling out and hanging in the night air behind it, a line I'd never really taken any notice of before. It went:

"Oh yeah, life goes on—long after the thrill of living is gone..."

I let the words register and they said what they had to say to a guy my age, a guy who'd lived the way I had. I ran my tongue around my mouth, letting it rub and nuzzle each chipped and broken tooth, each one telling me something about the things I'd done and the places I'd been. After a moment I got up and shuffled to the curb. The butt the kid had flicked lay glowing in the gutter, a good inch-and-a-half long. It cost me a little breath to bend down and pick it up, but no shame. I was all out of that. I hardly felt the old guy's stare as I put the still-warm filter—a Marlboro, pocked and blackened from someone else's sucking—to my lips and smoked it out. I couldn't even be sure if he'd turned to stare at me or if he was just looking past me, back east along Kingston toward the approaching bus, its headlights sodium-yellow, its signals and brakes orange and red, as it came hulking out of the night to gather us into its warm belly and take us downtown, to wherever we needed to go.

More praise for the 33 1/3 series:

We...aren't naive enough to think that we're your only source for reading about music (but if we had our way...watch out). For those of you who really like to know everything there is to know about an album, you'd do well to check out Continuum's "33 1/3" series of books.—*Pitchfork*

As individualistic and idiosyncratic as the albums that inspired them—Rob Trucks, *Cleveland Scene*

The best albums ever made—turned into books!—*Blender* magazine

This is some of the best music writing going on right now—*Pulse of the Twin Cities*

Music writing done right—*Tape Op* magazine

Admirable... 33 1/3 has broken new ground—*THES* (UK)

The series quietly breathes some life into the world of music fanaticism...an explosion of sincere, humbled appreciation—*The Portland Mercury*

The series represents the Holy Grail of millions of late Baby Boomers—*All About Jazz*

Inspired—*Details*

Neat—Nick Hornby, *The Believer*

A much-needed reprieve from the bite-size capsule reviews that rule much of today's music criticism—*San Francisco Bay Guardian*

Informed, fun and personal—*Paste Magazine*

The series tries to inject new life into a tired form—*Newsday*

All [these] books revel in the distinct shapes and benefits of an album, its ability to go places film, prose or sculpture can't reach, while capable of being as awe-inspiring as the best of those mediums—*Philadelphia City Paper*

These first few installments set the bar pretty high for those to come—*Tangents*

At their best, these Continuum books make rich, thought-provoking arguments for the song collections at hand—*The Philadelphia Inquirer*

A really remarkable new series of books—*The Sunday News-Herald,* Michigan

A brilliant idea—*The Times* (London)

The series treats its subjects with the kind of intelligence and carefully considered respect they deserve—*Pop Culture Press*

Lucid...each volume provides insightful commentary—*The Paper,* Central Illinois

Idiosyncratic, pocket-sized monographs done with passion and insight...the analysis is both personal and articulate—*Harp Magazine*

The series delves as deep as it's possible to go without resorting to padding...5 stars each—*Classic Rock Magazine* (UK)

Passionate, astutely written, and they lend real insight—*Amplifier Magazine*

If an enterprising college professor were to put together a course on pop criticism and classic rock 'n' roll records, the textbooks could clearly be found among the...33 1/3 series presented by Continuum Books. Each book delves deeply into an iconic album of the past 40 years, with a variety of approaches—*St. Louis Post-Dispatch*

Informative, thought-provoking, creative, obsessive and more—*Albany Times Union*

Articulate, well-researched, and passionate—*Library Journal*

A cracking good idea, and if you like the albums in question, you're sure to love the books—*Leaf Salon,* New Zealand

Eclectic enough that there should be something for everyone—*Maxim*

A nifty little string of books that deserves more attention—*Columbia Daily Tribune*

These little tomes have captured me in a gobsmacked haze...These writings are so vivid and uplifting—*Cincinnati City Beat*

Cultural elitism never had it so good—*Louisville Eccentric Observer*

Praise for indivdiual titles in the series:

<u>Meat Is Murder</u>

My personal favorite of the batch has to be Joe Pernice's autobio-graphic-fiction fantasia...Over little more than a hundred pages, he manages a vivid recollection of a teenage New England Catholic school life circa 1985, in all its conflict and alienation, sexual fumblings and misplaced longing—*Tangents*

Pernice's novella captures these feelings of the despair of possibility, of rushing out to meet the world and the world rushing in to meet you, and the price of that meeting. As sound-tracked by the Smiths—*Drowned in Sound*

Pernice hits his mark. The well-developed sense of character, plot and pacing shows that he has serious promise as a novelist. His emotional-ly precise imagery can be bluntly, chillingly personal—*The Boston Weekly Dig*

Continuum...knew what they were doing when they asked songwriter Joe Pernice to pay homage to the Smiths' *Meat Is Murder*—*Austin American-Statesman*

Pernice's writing style reminded me of Douglas Coupland's: the embodiment of youthful vitality and innocent cynicism, clever, quick-witted, and aware of the ridiculous cultural symbols of his time—*Stylus Magazine* (University of Winnipeg)

Forever Changes

Love fan Andrew Hultkrans obsesses brilliantly on the rock legends' seminal disc—*Vanity Fair*

Dusty in Memphis

Warren is a greatly gifted good heart, and I love him. Read his book, listen to his record, and you will too—Stanley Booth, author of *The True Adventures of the Rolling Stones*

Warren Zanes…is so in love with Dusty Springfield's great 1969 adventure in tortured Dixie soul that he's willing to jump off the deep end in writing about it. Artfully blending academic citation, personal memoir and pungent commentary from *Dusty in Memphis* principals such as producer Jerry Wexler, Zanes uses the record as a springboard into the myths and true mysteries of Southern life—*Rolling Stone* (4 star review)

James Brown Live at the Apollo

Masterful—*The Big Takeover*

Exemplary…Most astonishing, however, is Wolk's conjecture that to avoid recording distortion, the riotous album captured "James Brown holding back"—*Mojo* (UK)

Let It Be (Replacements)

These are solid short-short stories with bona fide epiphanies—that they shed light on Meloy's past only makes them more engaging—*The Village Voice*

For reviews of individual titles in the series, please visit our website at www.continuumbooks.com and 33third.blogspot.com